1157 PROPERTY PLAN

A Strategic Plan That Enabled Myself and My Clients To Build A Property Business with No Prior Knowledge or Property Expertise.

The 1157 Property Plan is Written With You In Mind and Will Show You, Guide You and Help You Create Your Six Figure Property Business.

Alasdair Cunningham

Copyright 2023: Alasdair Cunningham

All rights reserved

ISBN: 9798389069015

LEGAL NOTICES

The information presented herein represents the view of the authors as of the date of publication. Because of the rate with which conditions change, the author reserves the right to alter and update his opinion based on the new conditions. This book is for informational purposes only. While every attempt has been made to verify the information provided in this book, neither the authors nor their affiliates/partners assume any responsibility for errors, inaccuracies or omissions. Any slights of people or organisations are unintentional. You should be aware of any laws which govern business transactions or other business practices in your country and state. Any reference to any person or business whether living or dead is purely coincidental.

Every effort has been made to represent this product and its potential accurately. Examples in these materials are not to be interpreted as a promise or guarantee of earnings. Earning potential is entirely dependent on the person using our product, ideas and techniques. We do not purport this as a "get rich scheme." Your level of success in attaining the results claimed in our materials depends on the time you devote to the program, ideas and techniques mentioned, your finances, knowledge and various skills. Since these factors differ according to individuals, we cannot guarantee your success or income level - nor are we responsible for any of your actions.

Any and all forward-looking statements here or on any of our sales material are intended to express our opinion of earnings potential. Many factors will be important in determining your actual results and no guarantees are made that you will achieve results similar to ours or anybody else's, in fact, no guarantees are made that you will achieve any results from our ideas and techniques in our material.

No part of this book may be reproduced or transmitted in any form whatsoever, electronic, or mechanical, including photocopying, recording, or by any informational storage or retrieval without the expressed written consent of the authors.

ALL RIGHTS RESERVED

TABLE OF CONTENTS

Foreword	6
Introduction	9
Chapter 1	**15**
The Entrepreneurs Journey?	15
Chapter 2	**22**
Small Business Mistakes?	22
Chapter 3	**36**
Why Property?	36
Chapter 4	**43**
Playing The Game!	43
Chapter 5	**50**
1157 Property Plan - Ellen McDonald	50
Chapter 6	**69**
My First Property Deal	69
Chapter 7	**81**
Securing My First HMO	81
Chapter 8	**95**
Your Money Is In Your List	95
Chapter 9	**109**
Property Sourcing Business Setup	109
Chapter 10	**115**
Property Sourcing Compliance	115
Chapter 11	**122**
A Years Salary In Just Two Months	122
Chapter 12	**131**
Property Number Two In The Bag	131

Chapter 13 — **136**
    Which Property Strategy? — 136

Chapter 14 — **152**
    Real Life Case Studies — 152

Chapter 15 — **178**
    Getting Your Hands on The Keys Control vs Purchase — 178

Chapter 16 — **191**
    Getting Started On Your Journey! — 191

Chapter 17 — **195**
    Forget The Bull Shit and Just Get On With It — 195

Chapter 18 — **201**
    What's Your purpose? — 201

Conclusion — 210

Stay In Touch — 213

About The Author — 215

Foreword

The fact that you are reading this book suggests that you want to create a better life for yourself and you have chosen property as the way to do that. Well the good news is that you are in the right place. By reading this book you will learn exactly how Alasdair grew his company into the successful business that it is today and this book will show you what can happen when you stop listening to your limiting beliefs and instead start taking the opportunities that are right in front of you.

I remember when I first met Alasdair at a property event in 2021. He was on stage speaking about how he had grown his business from having very little to invest in property, to acquiring multiple houses each week for himself and his investors. As I listened to him speak about his life and his business I knew that I wanted to learn from him, but it wasn't just because of his success. Of course this did impress me, who wouldn't be impressed by what he had achieved in such a short space of time? However, it was the way he didn't solely talk about the successes but how he also spoke about his failures, his negativity and his limiting beliefs and how they had originally held him back from growing such a successful business.

This resonated with me because at the time, I myself, like many others, was struggling with negativity and limiting beliefs that were holding me back from success. So, to hear him tell the audience how he had been capable of pushing past it, made me realise that if he could do it, so could I.

As I listened to Alasdair it became clear exactly what type of person he was. Three things stood out to me, convincing me he was somebody that I wanted to learn from:

One, his success in the property industry.

Two, his genuine honesty.

Three, most importantly, his care and commitment to his students.

Like many of his students, Alasdair has helped me to not only grow as a person but also to grow my business and I am so incredibly grateful for the lessons that he has taught me.

If you want to be successful you need to not only invest in your education, but also invest in your environment and put yourself around people who have not only achieved what you want to achieve but who genuinely want to see your success.

Alasdair's sourcing company is just one of his multiple streams of income where he is averaging £35,000 a month from a list of just under 10,000 investors. He has shown that the power of investing in yourself and your education, has grown his business to a place where he has the time and freedom to do what he is truly passionate about, helping others.

He has spoken on stages across the UK, Europe, North America, South East Asia and parts of Africa, inspiring people to create the future they want, by believing in themselves, investing in their education and putting themselves in the right environment.

Alasdair has shown exactly what is possible, not just through his own success but through the success of his many students. By reading this you will see the exact steps you need to take, to achieve the same. He has helped hundreds of his students to set up and run successful businesses that are generating thousands of pounds each month. He has helped people to push past their limiting beliefs and completely turn their lives around. Many of his students are now running successful six figure businesses all because they listened and implemented the lessons that Alasdair taught them.

People are drawn to Alasdair not simply because of his achievements but because of his honesty, integrity and commitment to serving others. He is somebody that gives 100% to everything that he does because he genuinely wants to see people succeed. When you educate yourself and put his teachings into practice, he will be right there to celebrate with you when your success comes.

So keep reading and you will see how Alasdair overcame his limiting beliefs and the BS story that he was telling himself, to grow his property business to nearly 10,000 Investors. You'll learn the exact steps that he took to set up his business, going from his first deal to generating a year's salary in just two months. But most importantly you will see how YOU can get started and how property can become the vehicle for you to create the life that you have always wanted.

In later chapters I'll discuss how Alasdair helped me make my annual teachers salary in just one month after he taught me property and business, My business would not be where it is today if I had not taken the decision to work with Alasdair and this is why I am honoured to have been asked to write this foreword and contribute to the contents of this book.

I'm incredibly proud and grateful that Alasdair has named this book after my success, "The 1157 Property Plan" will be revealed in the coming chapters as to why Alasdair has named the book in honour of the success I have experienced as a result of working with his company. As you read this book please remember that I start as many of Alasdair's students started with very little to no property expertise or prior knowledge, in fact, when I started the number 1157 was incredibly important to me

Read on to find out more....

Ellen McDonald

Introduction

I've spent most of my working life believing that I had to work extremely hard for my money and that nothing comes easy, that's just how it is. I was always told "get a trade behind you" that way you'll always have "work". But I didn't want "work", I wanted a business.

To me "work" is code for a job and that's really not me. Some people love the security of a job, the predictability of a job and the life of a job. In fact you'll find that most people just want a good job for life. You know, the job they set themselves at school with the careers advisor to become a dentist, or bus driver or whatever they chose.

That's their goal, get a good job, earn a regular salary, get a house, get married, build a family, maybe if they're lucky have a few nice holidays, then retire with a nice pension to see them until they die. And that's honestly great if that's what you want, if that will make you happy and fulfilled then I applaud you.

It all sounds great doesn't it? But what happens when your "secure" job is no longer secure? What happens when the cost of living increases at a rate we've not seen in my lifetime? What about when fuel prices hit £2.00 a litre which has a direct impact across your whole life?

You see when you have a job, you're committed, you're restricted and you're controlled. So your nice life that we created a few paragraphs ago will surely start to fall to pieces. Soon it's not the life you imagined and dreamt of, and can very quickly become a monthly living nightmare. I'm sure you can relate to this because you're reading this book most probably because you're looking to escape the reality I've just mentioned.

Point blank there is no way I'm allowing anyone to control my future, my income, my time off, my success and my life, so I decided a long time ago that a "job" was not for me. One of the first things I had to understand was that I control my destiny and I and only I am responsible for making that happen.

We live in a world of "victims". What I mean by this is that for some reason there appears to be a generation with high levels of entitlement and expectation and if you fall into this category please give this book away right now. You'll be broke for the rest of your life and quite frankly I'm not interested in helping you. You must understand that you control you and your future. Own it and be responsible for that, the sooner you acknowledge this and own it, the better you will do.

Growing up I've always had an entrepreneurial mind. I was always thinking of new business ideas to get involved in. I remember being in my mid teens scouring the very early days of the internet (using dial up) to find new ways of making money, new business ideas, new products and opportunities and I came up with many. Some of which I made some money from, others lost me money. Every venture I entered into gave me lessons you'll never learn from school, as these lessons are life experience lessons.

It was late 90's and I had recently passed my driving test. My first car was a 1983 mini which I had been restoring for around 2 years prior in preparation for passing my test. The freedom I now have changed everything for me. You see, prior to this I would come home from work, jump on my computer and do what I could to learn, research and hustle, but now I've got the freedom to get out and about much easier which means I can start selling stuff much easier.

At the time I was buying items from a friend of mine called Kurt. He regularly travelled to Thailand, where he had a business and whenever he returned he would bring merchandise to sell to people like me, such as football shirts, trainers, jewellery and many other items. I used to buy popular football shirts off him at £6 each and then sell them around the pubs, carparks, industrial sites and burger vans for £20 each. Great little side hustle. I did this whenever I had stock from Kurt. This type of side hustle was the best sales lesson I ever got.

I had many little side hustles like this for many years. I always remember my parents once said that I would do anything to make money and whilst at the time that was correct, as I was selling fake items, I very quickly realised that I didn't want to go down that road after getting pulled by the police and having my boot and back seat full of stock taken from me. That day I lost around £500 worth of stock and I didn't really have that money to buy more. Although a huge setback for me, it was also a big lesson for me.

At the time, in late 90's and early 00's, I would agree with my parents, I would have done anything to make money, legal or not. However, after a few close calls with the police, I decided to step away from selling fake items.

Don't get me wrong, I know what I was doing was not strictly legal, but I pretty much guarantee everyone reading this book has done some sort of hustle in their life. Some of the stories I hear from my students are crazy, so it's all about perspective. I was just a naive teenager trying to make money.

The worst thing I ever did was sell fake clothes and jewellery. A few of my friends went down the route of selling other items, which never interested me in the slightest. Entrepreneurs are hustlers, you'll find we love the sale, the process and the feeling of making money. Some people take to obsession and can become very narcissistic over it and you need to ensure you do not go down this path.

I never did and never would. I agree with my parents, I will do anything to make money as long as it's legal, ethical and done with integrity. I tell you these stories to give you an idea of what the life of an entrepreneur is. Anyone that thinks they will make it on their first venture is basically delusional. Those success stories that you hear about first business successes are very few and far between and you're probably not getting the full picture. You will fail on your way to success so get used to it!

Since I began on my journey to creating a business, I've started close to 30 businesses, or opportunities and these range from buying and selling items, web stores, car rentals, minibus rentals, skip hire, bingo hall cafe, burger van, trailer maker, buying and selling cars, buying and selling karts and kart equipment, racing team, workshop business and franchise owner and more that I'm too embarrassed to talk about!

Each business has made and lost money and each business gave me unforgettable experiences and lessons and I wouldn't have it any other way. Those ventures made me who I am today. They created me, they created my skill set, knowledge, attitude, drive and motivation.

Back when I first left school my main career was as a mechanical engineer in the commercial vehicle industry. I chose this industry as I was always told "get a trade" behind you and so I did, and I loved it, I really did. Getting filthy dirty fixing commercial vehicles was great fun and again I gained huge experience during this time.

I was employed in a regular job working for a local bus and coach company and I worked shifts, either early morning or late in the evening, which became a little tiring and relentless. I was young and eager and starting to think what else can I do to make money and that took me to the side hustles we discussed earlier.

I was very good working with my hands, anything physical was no problem for me but I wanted to start playing smarter. On top of my wages I was making a decent side hustle income every week. As someone in their early 20's, I was making £400-£500 between my wages and cash from selling items. I always seemed to have cash around which gave me even more thirst for starting a business.

I always remember the day that I decided to quit my job. I was working at a stagecoach bus depot in Bedford and I was 22 years old. By now I was fully qualified and had completed a 3 year apprenticeship, plus I had considerable experience as I was always working on workshop duties but also breakdown duties. Trust me you learn a lot when you're trying to get a broken bus that's stuck in a service station in France, able to drive again, so you can take it back to base in the UK.

There were a lot of older engineers, 40 years and over and they had worked for the same company all of their career. They were so set in their ways and routines, many of them lived by a routine of doing as little as possible to get by and clock off as soon as they could. I hated this way of working and I couldn't do it. I've always been the type of person that does everything 100%, particularly when it comes to work.

The funny thing is these older engineers were only earning a little more than me, maybe an extra £40-£100 a week depending on how long they had been there. Even then they were mostly earning £400-£500 a week, where I was earning £350-£400 a week from wages.

So, I am in my early 20's and I realise that the most I can look forward to is an extra £100 a week after giving the company 20-30 years of my life. This for me was the realisation that I need to leave and do my own thing. It was a big wake up call for me that day, and that day I put a plan together to get me out of that depot as quickly as possible. There was no way I was staying here, everyone was miserable and all they did all day was bitch about money and life. As my favourite Rodney says "No Way Pedro"

Understand this, your network and environment will make or break you so you must control this. Over the course of reading this book I'll show you how I started my first legitimate business, how I scaled that to £400,000 a year in sales and how I recovered from near bankruptcy to becoming a successful property investor, speaker, trainer and Entrepreneur.

Let's crack on and get going.

Chapter 1

The Entrepreneurs Journey?

One of the biggest issues I've had to deal with is my self belief and confidence and I know many people suffer with this. It's something that I believe stopped me from really achieving success in the early days. Let me explain, I started my first business called "Headstart Engineering" in 2004, and to begin with I didn't have a lot of money. I had about a week or two's worth of wages kicking about and because of this I needed to start the business on a shoestring budget, which meant that I had to do everything myself. I couldn't afford luxuries like paying people to create marketing materials.

I started this business whilst I was working at Stage Coach Buses in Bedford by shifting my working shift to the permanent early shift. That meant I would have to leave home at 4.30am and I would finish at 1pm. I then had the rest of the day to build my business and try to find new customers. Everyday on the dot I would clock out at 1pm, jump in my van and head to whoever I thought may use my new mobile engineering services business. I visited all the bus, coach and lorry companies and any company that used commercial vehicles in Bedfordshire, Hertfordshire and Buckinghamshire. More often than not I was told to come back another time, or send me your information, and this rejection really started to dent my confidence. It got to a point where I actually couldn't cold call companies anymore because I would get all embarrassed and would just lose my nerve, so I stopped visiting them. I then moved to mail shots, sending letters, flyers and business cards in the post. It took several months of mail shots and direct marketing before I had any real interest in my services. All this time I was still working 5am - 1pm and then working on trying to start the business in the afternoons and evenings. As I wasn't gaining much traction I started to question whether I was making the right decision and those thoughts then compound. A little thought becomes a bigger thought which leads to a very down beat and demoralised Alasdair.

Keeping your head when starting a business is crucial because you will feel like I did. You'll question what you're doing and your friends and family may also question you about what you're trying to do, but you've got to remember why you started on your journey to change. For me this business was the first legitimate business that I had started, even though I currently had no customers, but it was a legitimate business, which was needed. I was passionate about it and I knew I could make it work so I just had to buckle down and get on with it.

And that's exactly what I did. I increased my mail shots, often sending them to the same company every month, and after months of doing this I started to get the occasional call. Now often these calls were more of a discovery call to find out what I could offer them, but either way I got the calls. One of these calls will soon enough be the call I've been waiting for.

It's now nearly six months after I first decided to start my own business, and I've done a few jobs for people and made on average £500 a month extra over this time. Not enough for me to quit my job yet but it's getting there. Time and time again I'd question if I should just bin it off but I kept going even though at times I was so frustrated and tired that I just wanted to break down. I've always said that you're only 1 call away from your big breakthrough, and for me, that call came from the owner of a bus company in Aylesbury, Chris. Sadly Chris is no longer with us, however, he had a long career as a multiple business owner working in the bus sector.

Chris had received my letters and was interested in what I was doing. He had done some due diligence and asked around the industry and found out that I was trained at a company called Seamarks Coaches and he had heard good things about me. Chris invited me over for a chat at his office in Aylesbury.

After an initial meeting Chris invited me to carry out the preparation on one of his buses for its annual MOT. The bus had been off the road for 6 months, and it had failed its last MOT. Commercial vehicle MOT's are not the same as your car MOT. If your car fails, you fix it and take it back with no real consequence but for buses if they fail, the operator is penalised and could lose operators licenses. Chris had already lost operators license and as a result, his business was being restricted from 28 vehicles to 15, which meant he was losing out on 13 vehicles making income on a daily basis which would amount to thousands a day.

Of course I jumped at the opportunity to take this job and I started on it straight away. We could take the bus for its MOT on Friday so I got straight to work on it. I did what I needed to do whilst trying to keep my job going, as I still needed the income from that. So I was working in Bedford in the mornings, travelling to Aylesbury after 1pm, working until late evening and then heading back home. Same again the next day and this was my life for some time.

Friday came and I took the bus for its MOT, and it passed first time. I expected it to so I wasn't really surprised but I felt a bit of relief more than anything as it meant I set a good example for my business and what I could do. I arrived back at the yard and as I pulled in Chris stopped to see how I got on.

I handed him the paperwork and said passed, no issues.

He just nodded, said "can you sort me an invoice" and walked to his office. I parked the bus up, gathered my tools and things and headed to my van to put an invoice together.

As I started adding everything up, the total was fast rising, before I knew the invoice was over £4000 and very quickly I had all these thoughts.

£4000, he's never going to pay that! You're crazy, he'll laugh you out the door, you're a new business, you've no credibility.

This is the nonsense I was telling myself and on that day I let the thoughts win, so I started to take things off the invoice. I thought as long as I make the same as my wages I'll be ok and I scraped the invoice to under £1000, which essentially meant I was charging him £10 per hour. My advertised rates were £45 per hour.

I told myself it's the first job for this customer so I can make the loss up later down the line of other jobs, anyway I headed over to see Chris. He greeted me with a handshake and said great job, very impressed and he pulled out the biggest pile of £50 notes I'd ever seen. Chris pulled out 6 notes and handed me them and said there's a tip. I'd literally not seen £300 in one go for a long time and I found myself struggling to hold back the excitement and I know it was only £300 but that £300 was a significant breakthrough for me.

I placed the invoice on the desk and said thank you and went to leave. He said "hold on, I'll pay you now". He took a look at the invoice, didn't even flinch, pulled out the cash and paid me in cash, in full, there and then. I asked if he's happy with the invoice amount and he replied "sure, I was expecting it to be around £5000!"

My heart dropped. I mean that's what the original invoice was meant to be. But because of my self doubt, lack of confidence and lack of trust in my ability, I sacrificed myself and £4,000, which at the time would be like me winning the lottery. Chris also handed me a list of bus registrations and dates, he said "you can do all my vehicles for the next 12 months, but Alasdair, charge me properly next time".

I just secured my first contract, and that contract netted me over £80,000 in its first 12 months. The lesson learnt on this was never to devalue what you can offer. Always trust yourself and trust your services. It all worked out in the end but it could easily not have. I quit my job the next morning, and gave my 1 week notice.

Fast forward 1 year and I'm no longer based out of a van. I've moved into my first workshop and have a mechanic working for me, multiple contracts and average £20,000 a month in revenue, of which profit is very high as it's service and consumables only. After a couple of years, now married with two beautiful girls, I grew this business to 4 members of staff and sales revenue of £350,000 per annum.

As great as it all sounds, the reality was that the business had lots of problems. As with any business, problems occur with cash flow, staff, work and customers and I experienced my fair share of these. We worked on terms with a lot of clients and some of these clients took 3 months to pay their accounts and as a small business we couldn't sustain this easily. Add this into staffing issues, and other issues and I was slowly losing my passion for this industry. I was working more and more and in reality, after all costs and expenses, I was only able to take a modest salary from the business each month whilst working silly hours keeping it going.

I had an offer from a staff member to take over the business some months earlier and I was now seriously considering the offer. Did I really want to be here for the rest of my life, working on buses and coaches? To cut a long story short, I didn't. So I took him up on his offer and he took over the business for a modest fee. It wasn't what my business was worth but something is only worth what you can sell it for, and I was happy as it allowed me to move into my next business venture. I wanted to create a business, not a job and with Headstart Engineering I had created a well paid job.

One of my friends was operating a franchise selling tools and equipment and he appeared to be living the life. I knew he was doing well and he was making great money and was doing this in nice clean clothes every day. He had also grown the business to multi operator so he had several vans in different areas doing the same which meant he could have time off and still be making money. This is what I wanted to do, make money while enjoying a holiday, or spending time with my family, not working 80 hours a week in a dangerous environment getting filthy dirty.

I used the money I made from selling my assets from the workshop to buy a franchise with the same company. I managed to get started very quickly as the area of Milton Keynes was available so I had been planning this for a few months when I knew I was selling the workshop. The first part of the process, once I had joined and paid for the training, was to travel to Dallas for the training.

It was a very intense training on how to run the business, how to grow and scale and most importantly how to become a master salesman. I loved this training and learnt a heap load of information about myself, my new business and how to grow and scale a business. I was eager to get started and as soon as I landed back in the UK I was taken straight to collect my brand new truck stocked with the best tooling and equipment on the market.

I hit the road and everything was going amazingly well. I was selling well, making money, collecting money, building rapport and clients, and honestly I was loving life. At the time this had been the best decision of my life, I'd never seen so much money, I was collecting £8,000-£10,000 most weeks and it just felt great having liquidity.

I had plans to take on multiple trucks and grow the business. I had a good business manager who believed in my ability and vision and my plan was to take 1 extra truck a year for 5 years. This meant I would be operating one myself and have 4 employees running the others and each truck would generate around £8,000-£10,000 a month after all costs so in 5 years I would have a very healthy business.

A great 5 year plan but as with all good plans there is always a but and here it is, and this is what nearly ruined me. You know, just when things start to go well in your life and you can start to see the fruits of all your effort and hard work, something seems to always go wrong and it's only recently that I accepted that the only reason it went wrong was down to me. It wasn't anyone else's fault except mine but at the time I was very bitter and resentful. This business taught me many things and here's what happened.

Chapter 2

Small Business Mistakes?

£4,320. If I wanted to keep my finance license, I would need to pay this amount on behalf of my customers who had failed to keep up with their monthly repayments for items they had bought from me. My business relied heavily on customers adhering to their contracts and if a certain percentage of my clients defaulted on their agreed contracted payments, then the finance company would restrict my account, which meant that my business would be unable to offer finance terms to the vast majority of my clients.

This would have been the third month in a row where I had to pay off bad debtors' finance, on top of all my monthly bills and expenses. This would sometimes turn into a roll on effect, if customers failed to pay more than one month, eating away at my profit. I had to do this if I wanted to continue to sell my products to the good paying customers.

It was a very frustrating position to be in considering 80% of the sales our business made were facilitated using finance or lease purchase. If I closed the month end with the finance book having more than 6% of defaulting customers, then the finance company would restrict my finance options for the next month. Quite simply this meant the end of my business. If I could not offer finance terms for the products we sold, the vast majority of my customers would not purchase. We sold high ticket tools and equipment and the only way most people could afford to buy them was if they could use finance options.

I needed to sort this out now, it had been going on long enough and my debtor's list was fast becoming a problem. My cash collections were lowering weekly and it meant I was struggling to restock. I couldn't keep running my business like this. The customers were laughing at me and quite frankly they didn't really give a toss that their actions were causing so much hardship in my business. To them I was just another rich businessman and could afford to bear their lack of payments.

As a business owner I feel it quite ridiculous that in the UK there is very little consequence for those who choose to pay their bills late and that needs addressing urgently. The whole system for non-payment of dues needs to be addressed and the power should be with the person owed the money and not the customer. After all they've had and enjoyed the product they bought, yet they can get away with not paying for it. It's ludicrous and criminal in my book. The biggest cause of failing businesses is poor cash flow, mainly due to non or late paying customers. Again I was facing cash flow issues very similar to those I experienced with my previous business.

Although the business was making money and profitable on paper, cash was drying up and drying up quickly. The business had stock and assets but an ever-decreasing bank balance, so our future was looking bleak. We could no longer facilitate bad customers' debt and we were now starting to run overdrawn every week. This is the sign of a failing business and you need to recognise when your business is going through this. It's brutal but you must acknowledge when cash is becoming an issue and address it quickly.

It stops today; no longer was I prepared to let customers take me for a ride, no more would I be paying their finance payments and then waiting months for them to pay me back. If a customer didn't pay me for their finance commitments then it would be on them from now on. They will bear the consequences, not me.

Because I had months and months of dealing with bad paying customers this led me to start resenting them. I had no time for them, which then meant I had grown to hate going to work and it became harder and harder to get the motivation to run my business. Putting in the effort to be polite to the bad payers was becoming increasingly difficult and my patience with them was wearing very thin. I recognised this issue and knew that I had lost my love for the business after just a few years. I was starting to feel trapped and bleak about its future. I was now at a point where there really was only one option.

I had to get out of this business and quickly, however, this was not as easy as it sounded. I had around £40,000 in outstanding finance payments owed to me by my customers - and that would take some time to collect in. I could write it off but that meant heavy financial losses for me and I couldn't afford to do that.

This was going to be a nightmare. I would be collecting this amount from customers, whilst serving the good paying customers and facilitating bad debtors, making the whole situation increasingly stressful and difficult. I was starting to hit a breaking point and really struggling to get my head back in the game. I needed to figure out a way forward and see if we could save the situation.

Christmas was fast approaching and I was looking forward to having some time off so I could stop thinking about the business and customers. The break was great but short. I actually felt quite rested after the Christmas break and decided to go back to work in the new year with the same attitude and positivity that I had when I started the business a few years earlier. Surely things will get better.

I spent a few days in between Christmas and New Year prepping my truck. Ensuring it was well stocked with new products and putting together offers and deals to help with sales. I spent time cleaning the truck so it was immaculate. I loaded some different toolboxes on board to give customers different options and made sure my truck was like heaven to a mechanic. Mechanics love shiny tools! 'Make them shine and they'll make them mine' we would say. The truck looked mint, well stocked, fresh and well merchandised.

I hit the road and arrived at my first stop of the day. Sales and payments were good. The customers loved the deals and the banter and mood was as you'd expect in a workshop. Things appeared to be like when I was smashing sales and really enjoyed the business so maybe it was me?

Was I the problem?

Maybe with a different attitude and mindset things might not be as bad as I was thinking? The first week after Christmas was a great week, we sold well above our average and finished in the top 20 in the UK sales within the whole UK franchise network.

Did I just need to change my downbeat opinion?

The rest of the month went pretty well sales wise and we got to the last week of the month, the week when customers' finance payments for larger purchases were due to be paid. Now, being January I expected a few defaults, but what happened made me realise that this business was no longer something I want to be involved in, let me explain.

The finance company allowed us a small percentage of defaulting customers without restricting my ability to offer new customers finance options. I took the decision over Christmas that I was no longer going to pay finance payments on behalf of my bad debtors and I didn't care about the effect on the business. In January I closed my finance account with nearly 30% default finance accounts from bad debtors.

This meant my business had restrictions on who I could offer finance options to - meaning I could only sell to those with exceptional credit scores. The vast majority of my customers were classed as subprime, customers with a few missed payments, but nothing serious like CCJ's or bankruptcy.

As with many situations in life, it's the few that ruin it for the many. Now, it wasn't the end of the world. If I opted to, I could still offer finance terms to those customers, however, this would be solely financed by my business and not underwritten by the finance company. This would be highly risky and I would open myself up to considerable financial losses if the customers didn't pay and this was not something I was prepared to do.

We were now into February and I was struggling with collecting the previous month's defaults from customers and as the end of February approached, this month's payments were becoming due. This whole situation was starting to become a bit of a nightmare. I was fast losing all interest in the business and seriously considering my next move. At this point I was losing money and unable to buy more stock. I wanted out of this and I wanted out quickly.

I made the decision a few days later that I'm out and this was my red diamond moment. This is a moment in your life when no matter how petrified or worried you are, you just go for it and say screw it, let's do it!

It was late in the evening around 9pm; I called my local area manager, Lee. He was a great guy, had served in the RAF for many years and joined this business on his retirement. He knew what I was struggling with as we had discussed in detail my issues over the last 6 months. This was the call he didn't want. I informed him of my decision to leave the business and as expected he tried to change my mind, but I was having none of it. He told me to call him back in the morning after I'd slept on it. I didn't need to - but I did out of courtesy. The decision was made.

From this point on, it felt like I had been released from prison. Not that I've experienced that, but you know what I mean. I felt trapped by this business, and now I was free.

The process of winding the business down started the very next day. I kept the news to myself for as long as I could, so I could pull in as much cash without customers using my leaving as an excuse not to pay. I stopped selling to anyone I knew would mess around with their payments and only bought essential stock to see me through until I finished.

We're now in the middle of April and I had pretty much wound my business down. I'd collected as much of the debt as possible and was not really working that much. By the time I had finished the business, returned stock and paid expenses, I had some money saved so I could afford some time off to allow me time to think about my next move. I would go out once a week collecting from the remaining customers who still had outstanding debts and to this day, I am still owed over £15,000 in bad debt; the chances of ever getting this are very slim.

The business taught me a lot of very valuable lessons, mainly not to deal in subprime lending or offer payment terms to those who cannot afford what you sell. I have no regrets in starting this business and likewise I have no regrets in leaving this business whatsoever as the business provided me a very comfortable living at the time - as well as many life lessons along the way.

I truly believe in "owning" your mistakes and failures; nobody else is responsible for your life. I completely shoulder the blame for allowing customers to take advantage of me; in the early days I was not strict enough, I allowed the late payments which initially were not that often but soon escalated and this was my fault. I guess the lesson here is *"give someone an inch and they'll take a mile"*.

Never again would customers dictate my business, income or happiness. The business is now closed and I no longer have anything to do with it. I have accepted I will never collect the outstanding debts.

Now, I am free to do what I want to do - but what do I want to do?

My problem was I have always been a grafter; I've always worked long and hard to get what I wanted. Apart from an annual holiday with the family, I rarely took time off, and now I had so much time on my hands, time to do whatever I wanted. This sounds great I know, and it was for the first few weeks, but then reality crept in.

What the hell am I going to do with my life?

I'm in my early 30's and surely this can't be it. I have no business, no job, no income and I was beginning to feel very lost. I was used to working and being out and about and now I was stuck at home with nothing to do and no purpose - and by now I was starting to feel very low and down. Being *free* was not all it was cracked up to be and I don't understand how people can go through their whole life without working.

I guess we all have low times and I'm nothing special. I don't deserve nor am I asking for any special care or treatment. In reality, I had a great life. I had a nice home, a beautiful family, no debt or real money worries, yet I was feeling completely worthless. I had become a very negative, sceptical, melancholy and down-beaten person. I had no interest or desire to do anything and my previous passions were now of no interest to me whatsoever. I'll happily admit I was not the most enjoyable person to be around. I was becoming increasingly tired as I struggled sleeping, 3 – 4 hours a night was the norm, which only added to my woes. I couldn't settle as my mind was buzzing with thoughts constantly, where did I go wrong? Was it my fault? What now? What the heck was going on with me?

Lisa, my wife, and I were in the kitchen and I found myself becoming emotional while having a chat about what I was going to do with myself. This is something Lisa had not really seen before, just then my children arrived home and came into the room; and of course, I tried to hide my face and not let them see me in this way. I didn't want my girls to see this side of me as I had always been the provider and rock for my family - and now here I was at my kitchen table and I can't emphasise enough the feeling of complete worthlessness I felt at this moment. My daughter Isobel asked why my face was red and what was wrong with me; Lisa made up a reason and ushered her away. I can't even remember the excuse Lisa gave.

I woke up the next morning, Lisa and the children had left for work and school and I was lying in bed, the hours had passed and it was now lunch time and I'd been laying there since Lisa left at 8am. No reason to get out of bed. I hadn't been out of the house for a few days. I remember lying there, watching rubbish on TV. I was watching a daytime talk show; on the show were two sisters, both addicted to crack and other drugs - and were so messed up to the point that they were living on sofas going from one drug den to another. What had my life become, that I was watching this crap on TV?

I shouldn't be doing this and I was going to sort this out today, so I decided to call and make an appointment with the doctor. Lisa had been telling me to go to the doctors for some time as she had spotted the signs of depression and anxiety - and so I finally took her advice.

I went to the appointment not actually knowing what I was going for. I wasn't sick. I'm old school and ignorantly believed that if it's not bleeding or hanging off then it's not broken.

"Mr. Cunningham, room 4 please"

I took a seat and was met by a new doctor whom I'd never met before. He was a very big guy, not fat, just well built and of a similar shape to Tony Robbins, but not as tall.

"How can I help you? Mr. Cunningham"

After a short pause…

I shifted forward on the chair, "I don't really know why I'm here, I'm sorry for wasting your time…"

I got up and walked towards the door to leave.

"How are you feeling?" He asked,

I paused for what felt like minutes and said, "I'm tired, very tired. I'm struggling to sleep and…"

Before I knew it I had completely broken down, I can't explain it. I remember being an emotional wreck. It was mortifying, I mean I was a grown man and I could not contain my emotions. I tried to tell him what had been going on, how I was feeling and I answered the questions he asked as best I could. I just wanted the ground to open up and swallow me whole. This was just not me. To open up like this to someone, a complete stranger was just not like me. I'm a man, we don't do this?

"Why do I feel like this? What's wrong with me? Am I just tired?"

I can't recall my doctor's name but he said:

"Mr Cunningham, you're suffering from depression. It's obvious to me".

What? There's no way I'm suffering from depression!

I ignorantly thought depression and anxiety was all in the head and that people just used this as an excuse. Now I know how that sounds, I'm the first to admit I was very ignorant about this subject. I now look back on this and realise how stupid I was thinking this.

The doctor spoke and I listened, he explained to me what it meant and how it controls your brain and feelings and that it's actually a chemical imbalance and not just *"in your head"* as I'd always thought.

Do you know what? I'm not the expert here so I was prepared to listen and take his advice. I took his advice and took the steps he suggested to try to regain some control and slowly I started feeling better. I started to regain a little purpose in my life and started to become myself again.

Now I was on the mend, I needed to start looking at my career and businesses as I was still jobless. I was not making any money and I was completely unemployable. I was running out of money quickly and my household bills were mounting up. I needed to create some income and I needed to do this quickly. I needed to pull myself together, stop blaming others and put my big boy pants on and get to work. Stop feeling sorry for yourself and get yourself out and back in the game.

I had a contact who had been asking me to work with him for a few months, assisting with commercial kitchen surveys for a new contract his company had recently won. Previously I'd said no way as it meant travelling all over the UK, but I decided to go for this -

even if it was just to get me out of the house and give me a bit of structure to my week.

I started working in his company and was travelling all around the UK. Getting out of the house was good and I was now earning a decent income so I could afford my bills again, which was a massive relief for me personally as it gave me back some self worth. I was slowly starting to feel normal and like a man again, being able to provide for my family felt good, actually just having a routine and working again, even if the work was mind numbingly boring, started to give me purpose. It's amazing how fast you will go downhill when you have no purpose or drive.

I believe things happen for a reason, now don't confuse that with me believing in luck, I don't. I believe you create your own luck in life and I had a massive breakthrough one evening when I was travelling around Wales for work. I often stayed in hotels and most nights I would be on the laptop trying to research and find new ventures, but one night I took a break and just watched TV.

There was a program called 'The Week The Landlords Moved In'. The program follows tenants and their landlords - and this week featured a landlord in his mid twenties who went to stay at one of his tenants' properties. Watching the program you could see the landlord had achieved considerable success in the property industry and I was fascinated with how he'd achieved this especially at such a young age.

What did he know that I did not know?

I was watching the program thinking how a 26-year-old has done so much in his life and here I am, mid 30's and struggling to make ends meet. I remember when I was watching the program thinking if I could just have an hour or two with him, he'd steer me in the right direction.

Whilst watching the program I did the usual "who is this guy?", so I googled him and came across his website. This led me to reading up on him – and I found that in less than a month he would be holding an event in Birmingham where we could meet him and learn all about him. I quickly booked on.

I remember Lisa rolling her eyes when I told her a few days later that we were attending this guy's event to learn all about property investing. I can't say Lisa was overly keen, but as the supportive wife, she agreed to come along.

We arrived in Birmingham to be surrounded by around 100 other attendees. We spent two long days learning all about property investing strategies and methods he had used to build his portfolio. I mean we were doing it, we were finding the deals, ringing agents, calling the letting agents to check for the demand, room prices and doing our own market research.

I've been to events like this before and have felt very uneasy as they generally are a massive sales fest from the moment you arrive to get you on another paid for event, so I was expecting some sort of further training to be offered. There is nothing wrong with selling an advanced level training however, but they first must give value for what you have already committed to.

As I expected, there was an offer to do further training on a 3 day training event, of course it's optional and it was not forced upon us at all. I was pleasantly surprised by this - as I expected to be getting sold too all day just the same as I had previously experienced. Anyway, I didn't sign up. My inner voices were in overdrive and I stupidly listened to them, negativity and scepticism slowly crept in.

"If he's so rich why is he selling you a course". I realise now that's the most idiotic thing to say. Why shouldn't he, why do people expect things for free? This is what I told myself at the time so I didn't commit.

Day 2 came around and it was much the same as day 1 but today was all about HMOs, lease options and other strategies - and for me, this was the best day. At the end of the day, he offered further training to anyone who hadn't signed up on the first day and again my inner voices were very active, but to my shock Lisa, (the biggest sceptic in the room) got my wallet out, handed it to me and said will you stop messing about and just go and do it.

We'd wanted to get into property for a long time and I thought this was the best chance we'd get. I took a moment and went to find out more. I signed up and this was the best decision I - or should I say Lisa has ever made.

This is how I got started in property, you see, for me I went through multiple businesses and failures before I started to see real success and the reason I share these failings with you is because I always wished successful people shared these instead of just sharing their success. This is what makes business real because every failing has taught me how to grow and run my successful property business and as we read on I'll show you exactly how I took my failings and;

- Became financially free from the income created through my portfolio of properties.
- Started a systemised property business which has an average income of over £30,000 per month passively.
- Utilised many strategies to buy or control property.
- Created a list of ready to buy investors who are looking to invest now.

- Became full time in property within a matter of months.
- Became a far more positive and confident person.
- Speak in front of thousands of budding investors every month.
- Helped 1000's of people through my training and sharing.

Chapter 3

Why Property?

Why did I choose property? For me it's simple, I like to see my investment. I like to be able to go and see my investment whether that be as a purchased asset or a controlled asset, so for me the only way I can do that is by investing in either business or property with physical assets.

Property is backed and can be leveraged and financed, you cannot legally borrow money to buy stocks or crypto currency. As of 2022 there is no lender that will lend you money to buy these types of assets. This tells me a lot, the fact that Barclays will not lend you money to buy Barclays stock says they are not confident in their own stocks. Yet almost every lending institution will lend against property. Now ask yourself why this is?

It's quite simple really, because it's a tangible asset that you can visit, value and have a future need for. Property will always be in demand due to the overwhelming demand for safe, warm homes and therefore the intrinsic value will generally always be on the increase. Now, that doesn't mean that the prices will not drop as we've seen in the past.

This is why I opted for property as to me it's the safest form of investment. Crypto currency, NFT's, stocks and shares whilst you can make a considerable amount of money playing that game, I feel property is far safer. However, I do have investments in these sectors. I've spread the risk of my cash across multiple different asset classes but by far property is the biggest for me.

Another reason I choose houses comes from family experiences and past dealing with bad landlords, having seen some of the poor standard properties that are offered. It shocked me that people accept this type of living, and like any business the property is your product so why not provide the best product you can. I really don't understand why landlords don't take pride in their properties as the returns will be considerably higher.

I guess these types of landlords are purely in it for the money and not to provide a high quality home for tenants. Happy tenants mean more profit, less void periods, less problems, and ultimately a more passive investment. I've always thought if we could offer a high-end property, then we would always have tenants.

Let's consider property in comparison to other asset classes and looking into property you'll find that most of the wealthiest businesses and entrepreneurs all invest in property and land, google Forbes rich list and you'll see that most of the top 500 are investing in property for long term wealth. They may have made money from business, however, they are investing the business income into property investments.

Take the McDonald's burger chain; we all know them for their fast food, but in reality, they are one of the wealthiest property owners in the world;

Former McDonald's CFO Harry J. Sonneborn, is even quoted as saying,

"We are not technically in the food business. We are in the real estate business. The only reason we sell fifteen-cent hamburgers is that they are the greatest producer of revenue, from which our tenants can pay us our rent."

For me property is the best form of investing. We live in arguably the most desirable place to live on the planet, with our net annual migration to the UK being in excess of 200,000. The UK boasts a booming job market, a wealth of technology, leading financial centres, big industry and a great multi-cultural environment where people can thrive and live a fruitful life, the opportunities are endless in the UK and this will always attract immigration. Also note that the country needs immigration, otherwise it would literally come to a standstill in a matter of months.

The population of the UK has continually increased over the decades, take a look;

2022	67.84 million people
2019	66.44 million people
2009	62.26 million people
1999	58.68 million people
1989	57.08 million people

As you can see there is a growth of nearly 4 million every 10 years and this trend shows no sign of slowing, so the need for affordable housing is always going to be there. Hence why housing is the safest form of investing available, now that's just my opinion and I'm happy to hear yours if you feel differently.

Now take the average house price taken from the UK house pricing index, you can easily find this online and this will show you the average house price for a two bedroom house in the UK. This excludes London as that is its own microclimate for housing which has seen incredible gains over the years, way above national averages. Just ask your parents and grandparents and they will most probably tell you about the properties they bought for literally thousands of pounds yet today, are worth hundreds of thousands. I know of many people who in the 70's, 80's and 90's invested into property and are now accidental millionaires because of the natural increase in valuation of these same properties.

This is a property my parents invested in December 1997, they held for 8 years then sold for £205,000 making a 204% increase. The property is number 79 St Margarets Ave, Luton, LU3 1PQ if you want to check the stats. Now ask yourself what else could you invest in that generates this level of return?

Sold	July 2005	£205,000
		+£137,500 (204%)
Sold	December 1997	£67,500

Statistically properties value will double every 10 years as history has shown. As we get closer to 2022 this is slowing. However, from when records began you can see that the average house prices has doubled every 10 years, then in 2008 the prices dropped overnight and then had a slow but consistent recovery.

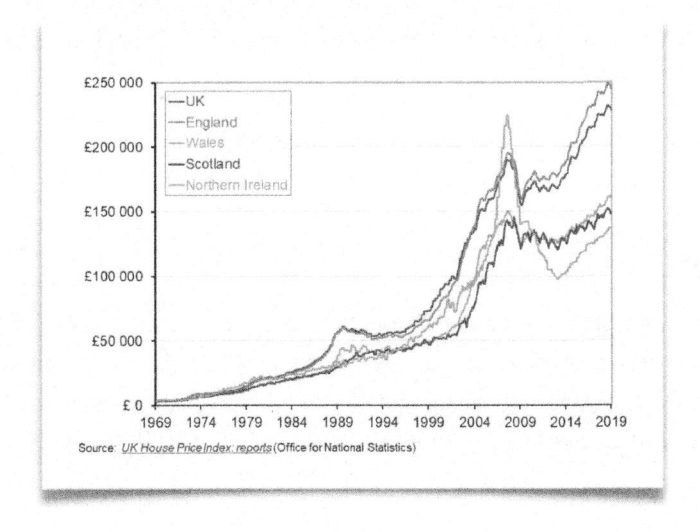

Average property price for a two bedroom house in UK

1970	£4,000
1980	£19,000
1990	£58,000
2000	£84,000
2010	£174,000
2020	£259,000
2022	£278,000

Even after suffering the biggest global pandemic of Covid-19 in March 2020 we have seen all time highs in the property markets. The last few years in the property sector has for sure been a sellers market.

The good thing about property is that no matter how far back you go, the pattern is very similar. So, by gaining the knowledge, you can ensure you are investing correctly and this will give you the absolute best chance to profit from property.

Let's say you have £20,000 in savings and it's currently sitting in a high street savings account earning as little as 0.06%; firstly, whenever anything starts with 0.0… I don't get very excited about this at all.

When you factor in the inflation rate of a predicted 11%, as reported by the Bank of England by the end of 2022, then your money is actually depreciating in the bank, and I don't mean it is less than when you deposited the money, I mean your £20,000 is worth less due to the increased costs of living and inflation. It will not get you as much as say it would have done a few years ago.

The UK in 2022 is seeing all time high living costs, with food, fuels and living expenses increasing constantly. Now at the time of writing this the fuel price is nearing £2.00 a litre for diesel, gas and electric costs are spiralling out of control and people are really feeling the pinch as we start to recover from Covid.

So, if you're in a position where you have money sat in the bank then the quicker you realise that it's actually depreciating then the better you will be. Today, the base rate for interest as set by the Bank of England rose to 1.25% but even so it still sucks to be a saver, especially when you realise that banks are using your savings to invest in property.

Here's a deal I found for an investor recently who had saved up for some years with around £60,000 to invest, The investor had two choices, they could leave it in the bank where in theory it would be "safe" and would accrue interest gain of around 0.06% or they could invest the monies into an appreciating asset which provided a positive cashflow on a monthly basis. Surprisingly, the investors decided to take a sensible risk and invest into a property with us and here's the numbers from the deal which we sourced for him.

Just looking at these numbers anyone can see that this is a considerably better way to invest and store his money. The return on investment is over 30% and after refinance the investor should only leave £12,500 of his own cash in the deal. This is a great example of the buy refurbish refinance method of accruing property.

BRR to Single Let

BRR			BTL ROI			Monthly costs	
Purchase Price	£115,000.00		New Value	£185,000.00			
Renovation	£30,000.00		Deposit	£43,750.00		Mortgage Payments (3%)	£328.13
Tax & legals 5%	£5,750.00		Profit made from refurb	£31,250.00		Management fee (10%)	£77.50
Total	£150,750.00		Mortgage amount	£138,750.00		Maintenance & Voids (5%)	£38.75
			Rent per room	£775.00		Utilities & bills	£0.00
New Value	£185,000.00		Bedrooms	1		WiFi	£0.00
Deposit	£43,750.00		Total rent	£775.00		Council Tax	£0.00
Mortgage	£138,750.00						
						Total costs per month	£444.38
			Money in Purchase				
Profit after works			Deposit minus BRR profit	£12,500.00			
New value	£185,000.00					Return on investment	
PP & Renovation	£150,750.00					Monthly cashflow	£330.62
Finders fee	£3,000.00		TOTAL	£12,500.00		Annual cashflow	£3,967.44

| Profit | £31,250.00 | | RETURN ON INVESTMENT % | 31.74% |

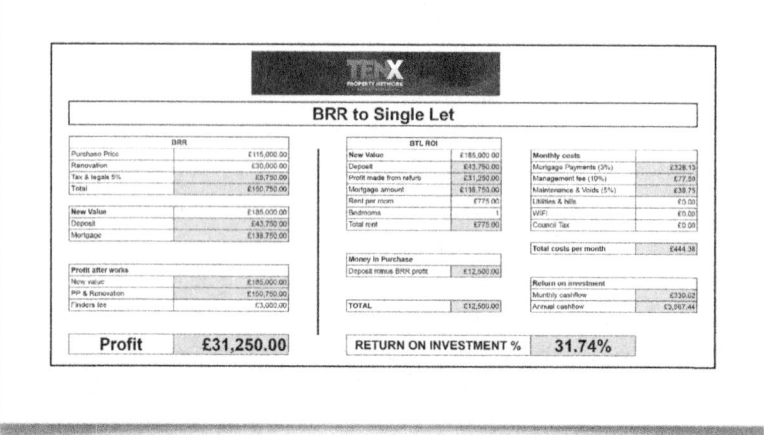

Even if things didn't go according to plan and the investor left £20,000 in the property deal, it would still be an amazing investment, far better than any return any bank can offer you, and this is why property is the number one wealth creator.

You gain cashflow and capital appreciation whilst being able to leverage the asset for lending against other assets, again tell me what bank will lend you money to buy stocks, crypto to shares in a business. You're right, none of them. As I said earlier Barclays won't even lend you money to invest in Barclays stock. That to me says a hell of a lot.

Hopefully you've made it to this point of the book and now understand where I'm coming from and why I've chosen property as the vehicle to both invest and create multiple business ventures from. Let's move on and start with how I went from the decision to execution. I'm sharing with you the steps and actions I took to achieve financial independence and create multiple six figure businesses on the back of my knowledge and interest in property, and here's how it all happened.

Chapter 4

Playing The Game!

You must take action. That's my biggest bit of advice.

You're not going to become a property investor by sitting on the sofa thinking and dreaming about becoming a successful property business owner and procrastination never got anyone anywhere so quit it right now. You've made a decision to read this book, so at least give yourself the gift of following it through and see what happens, and that's exactly what I did. I made the commitment to invest financially into my education around property and that gave me the drive to then follow it through.

Before you make any moves in property you need to first understand if it's something you really want to do, so get yourself along to some networking events and get to know the industry a little, meet people, build relationships and get some advice. When you've done this and are ready to go to the next level then you must get educated.

Do not even think you can do this to any level of success without education. Quite simply you will fail, lose money and give up, and I've seen this time and time again. Those who say I can learn that from YouTube, what you must remember is YouTube is there to wow you, show you what's possible and actually give you very little "how to" real life working knowledge so be mindful of all these guru's shouting about how great they are on YouTube. Whilst YouTube is great, YouTube is an entertainment channel designed to keep you engaged and in compliance so just be mindful of this.

Although I had some experience in property, I never really understood the property game until I started attending property related events. This is where I built my network and in turn my client base, get yourself booked onto high quality property events and go there with an agenda. What is your outcome? What do you want to take away from the event? Is it knowledge? Contact? Or a joint venture partner? I've gifted you two tickets to come along to my free property training events. The Property Accelerator is a great place to meet people, learn, network and get educated for free.

You can check out the website www.alasdair-cunningham.com for the next available dates and updates.

I booked myself onto some training and went along with high expectations, and although I'd invested what little money I had left I went with the right expectations for the training. I never expected a magic pill of success and I suggest you also have this level of expectation. I attended many training sessions by different providers, some of which were good, some bad and some excellent. However it's worth noting that I learnt valuable lessons from every provider, even if those lessons were how not to do something.

Training for me had to be the start as I am the sort of person that if I want to do something I become obsessed by it, so if I'm going to do this then I need to equip myself with the right tools for the job. Once I had attended some training I then started my search for potential property deals. I took the training and went with it, going through it step by step.

The first thing was to find a suitable area or goldmine patch, so for this I narrowed my search area down to Hull. After carrying out due diligence in Hull I then started the search for potential property deals that matched the property criteria I was working with. My specific criteria was any property that met the requirements for a good HMO opportunity, either as an up and running HMO or a property which needed converting.

I was literally spending every spare moment I had online searching for property deals, and over the course of a few days I shortlisted nine potential deals. These nine deals appeared to match the criteria and the initial due diligence I carried out returned positive results so I hit the phones and started speaking with the agents selling the properties. I managed to arrange a viewing on all nine properties but what was really interesting is if you just pick up the phone and start speaking to people, more opportunities will come out of that conversation.

One of the biggest lessons I gained from these conversations and viewings with agents is that property is more about the people and relationships you build than bricks and mortar. You will get so many more deals and opportunities by just speaking to people and building rapport with agents. They want what you want, remember that, they are sales people trying to sell property to whoever they believe to be the best possible buyer who can complete quickest. If you remember this when you're negotiating then you will get much better results. Give an agent what they want ie; a quick sale and they will flood you with deals. All they're interested in is making their commission on the sale and they will work with whoever can help them achieve the highest commission faster.

Another lesson I took from viewing properties and meeting agents and other investors is that you can spend a lot of time sitting at home scraping the online sales listings trying to find that needle in a haystack but when you actually just get out there you will probably find it much quicker. Action is what will set you apart from your competition. Even if the properties you are viewing don't work out you just never know who might be showing you around and what other opportunities they may have for you, and what I'll say is that the person who views the most properties, builds the most relationships and has the most conversations will definitely win this property game.

If you want to win then you need to ditch the excuses, and I've heard them all trust me on this. I hear daily from people as to why they haven't hit their goals and targets and every time I say the same thing, it's just an excuse.

The harsh reality is this, if you're not prepared to sacrifice something in order for you to achieve success in property then give up. You will fail. In order for you to grow and develop new skills, then something has to give whether that be your social life, friends, TV, nights out or sleep.

What are you prepared to sacrifice in order to play the game of property? When I first started in property I was travelling the country going to as many networking events as I could, sometime 3 or 4 a week and these could have been opposite sides of the country but I still made it to them, because you just never know what may happen or who you may meet, and the reality is most people are too comfortable in their life to achieve success. They think they want it but really they aren't prepared to do what I've done to get the success.

What I will say is that the property business is going to drive you crazy to the point that you will want to throw the towel in many times. It will drive you insane when all you hear is the word no thank you from landlords. You'll be rejected and told no more often than not so get used to it, and this will then make you question your ability, skillset and desire but trust me if you are driven enough to push through the failures and rejection you will reap the rewards.

Property is a game and you must play to win. I've called this book the "The 1157 Property Plan" for a reason because to me it is just that. This is a plan of real life monopoly where you can literally turn £1157 into £167,000 in less than 12 months just like Ellen McDonald.

When I first started in property I had enough money in the bank for one month's worth of household bills. I had very little in savings but I did have credit cards available which could afford me over £20,000. I had a great credit rating and no real debt but I wasn't in a position to invest cash into buying property at this stage.

Now, my cash holdings were not enough for a deposit for a purchase or for a small rent to rent deal, so I could easily have said to myself I don't have the money so I'm out. I won't bother viewing properties as there is no point. I can't buy it so what's the point in wasting time viewing the property. For many people this is a massive hurdle they need to get over, but for me I got over this straight away and I didn't let it stop me. I simply sold myself to the agents and what I mean by this is when I was asked how I would be purchasing the property I just said I would be looking to sell my home to fund the next property which is true and accurate.

You have to use what you have to play with, if you don't own your own home then you can't say this but think about what you can say which could help you become a credible prospect. Maybe you're working with an investor and you can use them for credibility, maybe you're on a training program like my property bootcamp and you can use me as someone you're partnering with in order to be taken more seriously. Play the game, remember that the agents are also playing a game of sales with you so you need to play the game of sales with them. It's important here that you don't do anything that would be untrue as you're trying to build a long term relationship but do remember in business everything you do is part of the sales process.

Now, because I played the game, I actually ended up securing a property using a strategy known as a lease option agreement. This property was in Melrose St in Hull and I managed to secure this deal by selling myself to the owners even though I didn't have the money to buy it. I'll cover exactly how this came about in a later chapter but for now just understand you never know what deal is around the corner and you must play the game of property in order to get these low money deals. This property generates a rental income of around £1,200 per month, of course there are bills and option payments to pay but even after all costs I still make a nice little side income from it and it cost me basically legal fees upfront of around £1,500 which I used my credit card to pay. There was an element of refurb to be carried out but I'll explain later how I funded this.

Some of the best deals will come your way when you're interacting with agents, get to know the agents; they will be your best deal finders. Over time, providing you do things correctly, you will become the 'go to' person for an agent when they have a deal to sell.

Remember property is about people.

The fastest way to build rapport with an agent is to buy from them, treat them with respect, turn up to appointments on time, don't mess them around and do what you said you would do. You should always treat their time like it is just as valuable as yours. I regularly get calls from agents I have dealt with because I am serious and someone who does what he says he is going to do.

Your Network is your Net-worth

Playing the game means you are building connections, getting to know people in the same industry, building a name for yourself and meeting other like minded people and this approach has provided me with a list of builders, painters, electricians and plumbers - and they are all from networking.

By playing the game of property I managed to secure my first deal using very little money but if I'd have told myself that I couldn't afford it then I would still be trying to get my first deal. Stop destroying your success by telling yourself negative thoughts because your thoughts lead to your feelings, which leads to your actions, which leads to your results so only positive thoughts are allowed in my world. When you come and join any of my programs we teach about positive affirmations, gratitude and positive energy and I know some you will be thinking that's a lot of mumbo jumbo and I used to think this too, but what I'll say is try doing the opposite for a few months and see how that makes you feel.

Tell yourself negative thoughts, negative affirmations and have a negative energy and see how far along and how successful you are after a few months. You wouldn't be in a very good place and you certainly wouldn't be very successful, so for the sake of your success please just be positive for at least the purpose of your own sanity.

Chapter 5

1157 Property Plan - Ellen Mc Donald

Let me introduce you to Ellen McDonald and the reason why this book is called *"The 1157 Property Plan"*. A former teacher earning £40,000 a year to a business powerhouse who's making on average £20,000 a month.

She achieved this in less than 2 years. Here's how she did it.

Ellen was a prime example of what can happen when you just follow the process without trying to reinvent the wheel. When I first met Ellen I was greeted by a slightly negative and depressed former teacher, yet I saw such huge potential. The problem was that Ellen couldn't see it herself yet, let alone believe it. At the time we met Ellen was on the verge of throwing her dreams away and returning to teaching.

She had reached a point in her fledgling property career where she had undertaken some training, however, was left with no clue on how to run the business and actually make money from the process. Her current business, if you could call it that, consisted of a couple of rent to rent deals, spread 100's miles apart. In fact, when we met, Ellen was in a position where she couldn't afford the rent payments due in the coming months.

This is the problem that I see time and time again when people undertake training and don't get the complete picture. They get 75% of what they need to make money and in Ellen's case this was clearly evident. She knew how to find a rent to rent, but she had very little knowledge of business and this is where she lacked. As she was experiencing these troubled times, Ellen was at a point where she was ready to return to her previous career of teaching.

Let's start at the beginning and uncover Ellen Mc Donald's story.

Ellen had wanted to become a teacher from a very young age. She fell in love with helping children when she was teaching ballet to local kids when she was a teenager. As a very creative young woman, she knew she was destined for helping people and in particular Ellen had a passion for working with children.

Conventional education through university taught Ellen to get a stable job. Specialising in English literature and History, Ellen was presented with a great opportunity to teach in the Middle East and work with children in Abu Dhabi.

What mid 20's young woman would turn this opportunity down? Especially as Ellen had fallen in love with the thought of working over in Abu Dhabi after seeing all the glitz and glamour on social media.

The decision was made and the plan was in place to make the move to Abu Dhabi. Initially she had the luxury lifestyle. The day began with a couple of hours of training in the morning followed by drinks by the pool in the afternoon and she was loving life. But after just a couple of weeks Ellen was relocated from her luxurious lifestyle to a rural fishing village, in the middle of nowhere. She had no friends, knew nobody, and had nothing to do apart from work. Things quickly became miserable for Ellen. The glitz, the glamour and the lifestyle that Ellen thought she would be experiencing very quickly diminished and all she was left with was her tax free £40,000 salary and a working for the weekend attitude.

You've got to remember that Ellen went out to work in Abu Dhabi to maximise her earnings as her goals were to build a cash pot so she could then buy a house for herself and working in a tax free haven was really speeding this process up.

Saving was the most important thing to Ellen and she was fortunate to be able to put aside nearly £2000 a month into her savings accounts. At £2000 a month, in just a few years her deposit would be very healthy and she could finally get her first property.

As most people do, Ellen thought the only way to buy property was to save up her money, use that for a deposit to buy a single family home, and rent it out. To get another property she'd have to start again from zero. While buying property in this way is a good idea, and it's certainly better than just leaving your money in the bank, it's a very slow way of growing your property portfolio.

Ellen knew that if she could make the most of her tax free salary, she'd be able to provide for her family. That's what was most important to Ellen, so she kept pushing and just dealt with the suffering she was facing. She could have easily just left Abu Dhabi and returned to working in the UK, but she knew that this would drastically slow her plan down.

She kept pushing through. She kept dealing with the kids even though they were badly behaved, and difficult to control. One of the things that kept her going was being able to visit Dubai every weekend to see her partner, as this gave her the taste of the lifestyle she wanted.

However, overall living in Abu Dhabi caused Ellen to completely lose her drive, her motivation, and most importantly, herself.

We're now in 2020 and Covid 19 reared its ugly head which meant one thing, Ellen was locked down in the apartment trying to adapt to teaching online.

It was around this time that Ellen's partner started learning about property investing as a business. They started watching videos on youtube and that's when they came across me being interviewed about property sourcing and they both became hooked on the idea. They watched a video where I discussed how I banked £27,000 in a matter of weeks by selling property deals to investors and whilst they found it really inspiring, it also annoyed them as they never knew you could make this sort of money that quickly.

They decided as a couple that as both of them were in lockdown and both were growing increasingly unhappy in the Middle East, a decision to return to the UK and pursue a career in property was on the cards, and that's exactly what happened. Ellen left her job and made arrangements to return to the UK.

I always remember the first time I met Ellen. She was a very quiet and underspoken woman who really lacked confidence. Now at this point I don't know if she's just shy or lacked confidence and self esteem. Looking back I now know it was a massive lack of belief in herself and this lack of belief or as I say "limiting belief" would be present for some time.

Ellen took some training and started implementing by securing a couple of rent to rent apartments, one in Cumbria and the other in York, both of which needed furniture, dressing and decoration which she undertook herself. After the set up and work required Ellen would have been making £700 to £1000 per month.

She managed to negotiate that she got a 2 week rent free period so she could decorate the property, as well as paying no deposit either. This was in exchange for painting the property and replacing the sofa. Once again, Ellen used exactly what I had shown her. I teach all my students that you don't need to pay deposits for properties as long as you can provide value to the landlord. An example of this value might be that they get a free couch, or you might do a light refurb on the property. This is your chance to get creative, and start thinking outside the box.

So Ellen collected the keys and got to work. The property needed to be staged so that people would actually want to stay there. She booked a photographer for the property, but she didn't have time to use him because the day she completed the staging, the property took a booking for a guest visiting for York Races.

No sooner did that booking come in, another booking came in for the week after, and this was a month long booking. The man who booked the property was working for a glass company in the area and the company kept extending his work with them. By the time he left, he had stayed in Ellen's property for 5 months. That long term booking gave Ellen a profit of £810 a month for those five months. Great deal, right?

Yeah it definitely was.

Business appeared from the outside to be great, with two properties under her belt, money coming in, the search for more deals continued. Due to the fact that the properties were spread out and Ellen was focussed on two areas which were several hundreds miles apart the stress was starting to show.

One of the problems with the business was that it wasn't just Ellen and her partner who were in the business but also her partner's brother. This was great for spreading out the workload, however, that's three people who want money from the fledgling business. Now as many know cash and cash flow is what keeps your business afloat, without it is like draining the blood from your veins.

The pressure of multiple properties for themselves, the property sourcing business and the need for enough income for three people started to show signs of winning. I mean there were times when Ellen was robbing Paul to pay Peter, using credit cards to get by and trying everything to make all the payments required to stay afloat. It didn't matter how much money they made, there was always something that took it back.

That's not a business, that's a very heavy weight on your shoulders, and Ellen was starting to realise that.

There had to be a better way. There had to be a way for Ellen to be able to support her family like she was able to before she came back from Abu Dhabi. She knew that business was the way to do that, she just needed to make some changes.

Little did she know, there were some massive changes on the way.

Ellen came to her first Tell The World in October 2021. Tell The World is my signature 4 day programme, and it's designed to show you how you can become the biggest, most confident version of yourself you've ever been.

Her experience of Tell The World was like many others. She was a little unsure of what to expect but over the course of the 4 days we spent at Tell The World, Ellen slowly started to open up and reveal her inner strength. You see, Tell The World is designed in a way to slowly build you up and make you a power house and Ellen took to it like a duck to water.

Ellen's experience at Tell The World was one of revelation. Her true self was able to emerge and the inner power was able to come to the surface and be present. Ellen left Tell The World a different person and almost immediately she started to see a difference in her business. This is when Ellen decided that if her experience of Tell The World was that great, just imagine what could happen spending a whole 12 months with me, so she made the decision to join my Business Academy.

Ellen then had a very rough start to 2022. In early January 2022, Ellen's grandfather passed away. This hit her hard because he was her biggest supporter. He loved seeing Ellen running her own business. He loved hearing stories about how the business was going, and what she was learning from running her own business, and I think he was, and still is a massive source of strength & inspiration for Ellen. She was doing this to make him proud.

We were approaching the next Tell The World event and this was just a few days after Ellen's Grandfather's passing, and while Ellen was grieving, she knew that she just had to be at Tell The World. She knew that Tell The World would give her some of the tools she'd need to be able to deal with her Grandfather's passing.

I would've happily let Ellen miss this Tell The World, but I don't think I could've stopped her coming along. She was coming for both her, and her Grandfather. Tell The World gives you opportunities to dive deep, and seriously reflect on your situation, and thankfully Ellen was able to get a LOT from that event.

The first major realisation that Ellen got was that she needed to do things on her own. She had had enough of not having full control in the business, enough of not being able to make the decisions, enough of not getting all the money. That was huge for Ellen because not only did it mean she was going to have to leave the business that she had created with her partner but she was also going to have to end a 3 year relationship. That's never an easy decision to make, even though it was the best for them both.

The second major takeaway that Ellen got from that Tell The World experience was that she needed to start building a legacy in remembrance of her grandfather.

Now's the time to make it happen.

Now's the time to do Whatever It Takes.

Now's the time to make her family proud.

This time she's doing it on her own. This time she's doing it her way.

Ellen was in the perfect position to start her own business. She now knew how the business ran and was able to learn from the mistakes of the first business partnership, and she had experienced what being a Businesswoman felt like, and she liked it!

It was just a different level of vibration this time.

Ellen took a month to properly process, and accept her Grandfather's passing and in that time did all the boring compliance side of setting a business up like setting up a limited company, getting bank accounts open, insurances and paperwork.

Then, on the 16th of March 2021, Ellen met me in Central London for her first Business Academy one to one mentoring session. Ellen had intentions of just getting a clear plan that day, a clear road map to get her to financial independence but what happened on March 16th 2022 will shape and change Ellen's life forever, and this is where 1157 comes from.

Let me explain..

1157 or should I say £1157 is what Ellen had in her bank account that day, now some of you may be worse off than this but bear with me. That £1157 was accounted for, as rents on her properties were due and the amount required was nearly double the amount she had in the bank, so actually she was in negative.

I've recently found out that on this day Ellen had actually borrowed her sister's credit card so she could pay for the train tickets and underground tickets, it was also the case that Ellen couldn't even afford to buy food and drinks on the day. Ellen was literally on the breadline with no clear path forward.

Now here's where things start to get interesting. I never knew any of this, as far as I was concerned Ellen was doing ok and was coming for a fairly normal one to one meeting. What happened over the course of the next few hours changed everything for Ellen and I mean everything.

As her one to one started, we worked through Ellen's goals and targets and part of it has to be about assessing her current situation both financially and personally.

After full disclosure of her business and properties I explained to Ellen that if she continued with the current plan then she'll be completely broke in a matter of months if not weeks as the business was already cash poor but also haemorrhaging cash every day.

I advised Ellen that in order to clear her path and create a workable and profitable business then she would need to restructure her business, her properties and her daily activities in her business. She was a busy fool, earning less than minimum wage and cash poor.

I advised that although the properties were individually profitable they were badly positioned due to the geographical location and self management which meant they were heavily reliant on Ellen's input.

My advice was that she sells the property deals to an investor so she can regain some cash in the bank and relieve her of the stress of running the properties. I advised Ellen to hammer down on one area, and dominate that area. To do that, Ellen was going to need some money in the bank.

Ellen reluctantly agreed after some persuasion, however, was very sceptical about whether or not an investor would buy these properties. They were both up and running properties with future bookings so actually very attractive for an investor.

So we drafted the email and sent it out to my database of investors and continued with the mentoring session. As I was speaking with Ellen I could see that she wasn't fully present, she was distracted and I quizzed her on this.

"Who's going to buy these deals?"

I mean seriously, who would pay the fee for the deals and take them as they are?

All these limiting beliefs were going through Ellen's head.

How much will I actually get from the sale?
What will Alasdair keep back for access to the investors?

And just as quickly as these thoughts were entering her head and taking her out of the game, I started to get text message after text message from my investors.

"Yes, Property 1 and 2"
" I'll take both properties, call me asap"
" Yes"
" Property 1"

And so on and on and on. Text after text after text… within 1 hour I had over 20 text messages from investors from all over the world, all wanting to proceed.

I let Ellen wait for a bit and we continued with the mentoring, and during this time one of my trainers Tom Cooke who specialises in the planning and business side of things joined us for lunch. We as a group put together a clear plan for Ellen and this plan relied heavily on the two property deals we promoted being sold on.

The time came to start calling investors and what happened next blew Ellen's mind wide open. I think deep down Ellen did not believe they would sell and if they did then the process would take days, but what actually happened was both deals sold to the first two phone calls I made.

You see I've mastered the art of selling property deals and I am confident that I can sell any legitimately good deal to an investor in a matter of minutes. Ellen witnessed this first hand as we sat in the bar at the hippodrome casino in central London.

The first deal was sold to an investor called Callum, who was currently skiing in the french alps and currently on the slopes. The other deal was to an investor called Ivan, both were serious investors with money to invest and both looking for an entirely hands free opportunity.

The fee we charged each investor that day was £8000 for a fully turn key rent to rent deal. The investors were happy and both paid the full fee within the hour.

Both Investors paid directly into Ellen's bank account taking her account from £1157.81 to a staggering £17,157.81 in just a few hours.

And here's the thing...

I didn't ask Ellen for a single penny. The whole amount was for her to keep and the reason I did this was because I wanted Ellen to for once in her life know what it felt like to have money in the bank and also to see what is possible when you start to believe.

I say to all my students " when you see it you cannot unsee it" and Ellen just saw her future.

She didn't even see the money.

She saw what was possible because I just proved everything she had heard people talk about.

Ellen says that day wasn't about the money, it was about her realising she could actually do it. That day opened her eyes to what her own business could look like. It showed her that she truly could do it.

Looking back, that was a massive turning point for Ellen, and it's definitely changed her life. She's never going to be able to unsee what she saw that day. She's never going to forget how she made half her annual teaching salary in a day.

Ellen went to see those investors at the properties the next week, and in her head, she was still trying to find ways it mightn't work.

That's why you can never stop working on yourself, and your mindset.

But to her surprise, both the investors were over the moon with the deals. They were both London investors, and didn't care about where the deals were, as long as the numbers worked, which they did.

In fact, the investors were so happy with the deals, that one of them agreed right there to buy another 4 deals from Ellen and instructed Ellen to find them as soon as possible.

Ellen phoned me asking me what she should do as they were my investors and I have a rule in my business that if I introduce you to an investor then it's a one time deal only.

I appreciated Ellen informing me that my investor wanted more deals because for me integrity is everything. Callum committed that day to a further 4 deals costing £8000 per deal and paid Ellen a bespoke sourcing fee on the day

She invoiced the investor for 4 Bespoke Sourcing fees, which were worth £1,500 each. The full fee for each of those deals was £8,000 each too.

In just a matter of days after our one to one mentoring Ellen generated £48,000 in sales, of course there are costs involved and this is not all profit however, the profit margin is very nice.

She was earning £40,000 a year in Abu Dhabi, and then she skyrocketed to making more than that in 6 weeks. Now of course, there's some costs to that, but that gave Ellen the belief she could run her own business, that she could deal with investors, that she would be able to provide for her family, and most importantly, that she'd be able to make her grandfather proud.

Ellen took my advice, and went from strength to strength in business. Instead of going all over the country, looking at whatever she could, Ellen decided to focus on one strategy in one area.

Ellen focused on finding R2SA deals, both for her investors, and for herself. She used the money from the deals she sold to fund her own deals. Ellen's now got multiple streams of income. She literally rinsed & repeated because she knew the system worked.

Ellen now has a business which is thriving and making sales each and every month bringing in over £100,000 in sales in less than 6 months and at time of writing this book her total income in less than 12 months is over £180,000

Building a six figure business was a major achievement for Ellen. The first time you hit 6 figures in your own business is always a huge milestone.

But hitting six figures in business meant more to Ellen than achieving it. The reason why it meant so much to Ellen was because she finally got to tell her Dad that she had hit six figures. I spoke earlier about how much of an inspiration Ellen's grandfather was, and is, to her.

Her Dad was just as much of an inspiration.

Ellen's Dad had his own bookmaking business for her entire life, and that's what Ellen grew up around. She grew up seeing that if you do it right, you can use the business to provide for your family, which is why this was so important to her.

Ellen's Dad sold his book making business after several decades in the business, so that he could move onto something else. Unfortunately, in between when he sold his business, and getting to start another business, he fell quite ill, and was no longer able to run a business.

This caused Ellen to want to take on the responsibility of providing for the family, just as her Dad did for many years. So for Ellen to be able to tell her Dad that she had hit six figures, and hear how proud of her he was, meant more to her than any amount of money.

To celebrate hitting six figures, Ellen took her family to Prague. It had been their family tradition for many years to go to Prague for the horse racing. They hadn't been able to go for a few years. This is what having her own business did for Ellen and her family.

A lot of people take their foot off the gas when they reach major milestones, such as hitting 6 figures in business, but not Ellen. Ellen was determined to finish the year strong, and that's exactly what she did. Ellen focused on finding great deals for her investors. She kept it simple, and because she offers such a good service, pretty much all of her business comes from repeat customers. Even better than that, her repeat customers keep telling their friends how great she is, so now Ellen has investors coming to her. She also has landlords, and letting agents coming to her because they were so happy with Ellen when she had worked with them earlier on in the year.

That's the thing about the Property Industry. It's a people game, and people buy from people.

Ellen went full throttle for the rest of 2022, and finished the year on a high. In the first 8 months of Ellen having her own business, she had turned over £147,000.

Quite an achievement, right?

Just think about how much your life could change if in your first year of business, you could turn over nearly 4 times your previous annual salary. Think about how different life would look, and how you'd be able to provide for your family.

Ellen has continued this good run into 2023, and she now has new problems in her business. Ellen's biggest problem is that she has too many investors, and not enough deals.

In fact, the investor that bought 5 deals from Ellen when she was getting started, has committed to buy 20 deals from Ellen this year.

Yeah 20 deals, and he keeps bringing Ellen investors as well. These are the types of problems you should want in your business.

Too many customers.

Because when you're in such demand, you're not desperate to sell to someone. You can actually fire your customers.

Ellen's business has grown so much that she's now taken on her first full time member of staff. She's also started helping me inspire women in business.

I've had Ellen speak at a number of my events, and she even came to Vietnam with me to help teach, and inspire out there. She's now an international public speaker, and is quickly becoming a world class speaker.

Ellen has also agreed to help me run a Women In Business seminar, which is aimed at encouraging, and helping women getting started in business. All of this growth and success has come from the last 12 months of Ellen putting in the work, and meeting me halfway.

I say to all of my students,'Meet me halfway'.

Ellen met me halfway, and now she's in a position where she feels broke if her business doesn't make at least £20,000 a month.

She's on track to hit a Quarter of a Million Pounds in turnover this year. Ellen is also planning on buying her first property this year.

This is only the start of the legacy Ellen is building and in honour of her commitment to her business and me I have named this book "The

1157 Property Plan" to inspire you that no matter where you are you have the opportunity to emulate Ellen's success.

Chapter 6

My First Property Deal!

I invested the majority of my available money into education which meant I wasn't left with much money to invest and now more than ever I needed to be creative with what I had if I wanted to be successful. After I had attended many different training events I had gained a considerable amount of information and knowledge and now was the time to take the knowledge and put it into action, and that's exactly what I set out to do. Action was the key word that I took away from the training. We had been shown so many success stories of how people had come from similar backgrounds with similar amounts of initial investment and gone onto make their full time income or indeed become financially independent from property income, so it was definitely possible but one thing all these success stories had in common was that they all took serious amounts of action.

So as committed as ever I set out to view as many properties as possible and meet as many people as possible over the next few weeks. In my head I knew that the more agents and investors I spoke to then the more opportunities would come my way so I set about identifying my goldmine area that I would start my new property business in. I followed the training and coaching and started out by shortlisting areas that were within two hours of where I lived. Those shortlisted were all areas that were busy areas, ideally cities of popular locations with good amenities, schools, hospitals and ideally a university and the shortlisted areas were;

Sheffield, Nottingham, Doncaster, Grimsby, Birmingham, Corby, Wolverhampton, Kettering, Peterborough and Hull.

I then carried out further extensive due diligence on these areas and realistically probably spent a few days doing this. I was checking for things such as supply and demand, local rules and regulations, HMO rules, stock levels, demographics, crime statistics and potential area growth. All this is to determine whether or not the area is suitable for a longer term investment that would not only provide good cash flow but good steady capital appreciation of the assets. I spoke to lots of estate agents and letting agents to get their feedback and opinion on the areas to invest in and the areas to avoid. Be mindful that there are many agents who will try to sell you a colour coded map of the areas, which detail the good, the bad and avoid areas of your chosen location and it's up to you if you invest in these maps. I never did, instead I chose to do my own area due diligence.

I finally chose the area of Hull on the east coast. I chose this area because it had recently received the award of the EU City of culture and as a result this included a hefty injection of cash to regenerate the area. Now the exact figure that the City of Hull benefited from is not clear, however, reports suggested that the overall benefit was in excess of £880 million worth of investment, jobs and infrastructure upgrades. You also had the docks, working port, along with the University and teaching hospital which would always provide a steady flow of potential tenants and workers in the area looking for short and long term accommodation.

Now I had my area, I needed to get myself known in the area and that meant networking and speaking to as many people as possible in the area, and the first thing I did was book myself into the next local networking events, so all I did was google networking events in hull and up popped every networking event happening in Hull for the next few months. I booked myself onto all the events that I thought would serve my agenda. After this I hit the streets and started walking into estate and letting agents to have conversations that may lead to any potential opportunities.

To be honest I really struggled with these walk in meetings and if I'm totally honest I was suffering from incredible imposter syndrome. There's me in an estate agency talking about property investments and I'm a complete beginner. I'm sure you can relate with this and I'm sure you've also experienced this. However, what I'll advise you to do is just be confident, fake the confidence if you have to, but be confident even if you're trembling on the inside. You must not suggest you're more successful than you are and you mustn't lie about who you are, for instance don't go into the agency pretending to be a successful investor with multiple properties as they will see through this straight away. If you want to be taken seriously it's all about credibility, honesty and doing what you said you were going to do.

The conversations went well with the agents and actually provided some great relationships and potential opportunities, surprising really as I didn't really have much money to invest so I wasn't really holding much hope of securing any sort of decent deal, little did I realise that if I'd allowed my self sabotaging beliefs to stop me doing the walk in visits, then I would never have secured my first low money down deal. One of the agents managed to arrange a few viewings on suitable properties in the area, now this business is about to start getting real.

The next day was my first day of actual property viewing and I'll always remember this day. As I arrived at the first viewing around 9:15am, I was met by an agent, a young woman called Beth. She was lovely, very helpful and friendly. Beth was employed to show people around properties and on that day she had 16 viewings to carry out so Beth was busy that day. I had built it up in my head that estate agents and those showing you around viewings were all experts in the field and that made the viewings that little more intimidating, however, I was pleasantly surprised that in all honesty, Beth, as lovely as she is was not the property expert I imagined her to be.

Actually, many estate agents and viewers are in fact sales people, the vast majority of them actually have very little knowledge of property investing. They are often not investors but they can show you the house and can inform you of the property, as I said not all are like this, but many are - and this was a real eye opener to me. I've met some amazing agents and viewers and some really successful property investors that own agencies. The reason I tell you this is because I really built it up in my head that I would be this naive, new property investor and I would be judged and looked down on when in fact I was actually the person with more knowledge.

At the first property I viewed it was a group/open viewing which meant there were many people viewing at the same time. I was happy with this as I felt a little intimidated during this viewing. I cracked on and did the usual property checks, checking the overall condition, was there any damp? What were the electrics like? What was the boiler like? Literally I was going round checking everything I could. Now this property needed a lot of work and I knew it wouldn't work for myself - but I was trying to be a property investor and I was trying to be taken seriously so I asked the right questions, said the right things and suggested I was interested. In reality I was not interested but I just wanted to play the part. If you want to access my free property viewing guide you can download it for free at www.alasdair-cunningham.com.

Now, I don't really know why I didn't just say it's not for me and move onto the next viewing. Looking back at my early mistakes I realise it wasted an hour of my day, where I could be searching for better deals or building more relationships. The viewings I had for the rest of the day pretty much followed the same path as the first property, mostly properties in a dire state of repair with a ridiculous amount of work required to make them fit for rental. I did have another day of viewings booked in Hull so I found a hotel and waited in anticipation for the next day. Hopefully we'll find a great deal on this trip.

The next day's viewings consisted of me viewing a range of properties with a huge range of problems including excessive damp, subsidence, flooded foundations and structural issues, basically another day the same as the first with little success and certainly no properties that were good enough for me to source for investors to buy.

It's funny because if I knew then what I know now, these properties were actually all potentially great investments if purchased correctly and they all would have been amazing for the buy refurb strategy.

Day two was a busy day with nine properties booked to view, unfortunately I never managed to get round them all as I spent far too long in each property, which meant I ran out of time. It's important that if you're running late and know you'll be unlikely to make an appointment then please ensure you let the agents know about it, their time is just as important as yours.

Fortunately for me all the missed viewings were able to reschedule to the next day so not all was lost. Communication is the key here so make sure you stay in touch with the agents. It's very important to have a great relationship with agents, so always keep them informed and up to date if you are running late or if you are going to miss an appointment.

Off I go to find another hotel for another night stay in Hull, I hit Right move in the evening trying to find some more potential viewings for the next day, being honest I was actually getting a little deflated this evening as I've now had two days of viewings and have nothing to show for the efforts I've put in. I did pick up some lessons however.

Firstly, I learned not to waste time in properties that clearly didn't match my criteria, this is not productive and is a drag on resources and time and secondly I realised how important it is to treat estate agents well. I witnessed an investor being very blunt and rude to an agent just because she wasn't sure of local rules. The viewing agent wasn't a property expert, she was just showing people around a house and this guy was being a complete tool, there's simply no need for it. You will only alienate the very people who are trying to help you. The estate agent should be your best friend, look after them and they will return the favour. I now regularly get passed off-market deals from agents I have dealt with because I treat everyone with respect, fairness and equality. It's so important to build good relationships in this industry. Being a successful property investor is as much about people as it is about bricks and mortar.

Day 2 arrived and I got to my first viewing at 10am, the property was a 3-bed terraced property just next to Hessle Road in Hull, looking at the link and images on line gave me a good feeling about the property, the asking price was just £90,000 for this 3-bed terraced in a great area of Hull for investment.

I arrived and was promptly met by Ian, a local agent who was showing me around. We had a brief chat outside about what I was doing and what deals I was looking for before we headed inside. Now so far in Hull all I've experienced is wrecked properties needing a lot of refurbishment work so this property was looking to be a better prospect.

As we entered the property I knew straight away it was looking to be a good deal. I was asked to remove my shoes as the property had recently undergone a full refurb so that's always a great sign. The property was fully refurbished from top to bottom, I mean everything was new from the flooring to the electrics, literally everything was new inside, this property was the real deal and the owner has obviously invested a fair amount of money and time in making it to this standard.

All boxes were being ticked with this deal, the price was right, the room sizes were perfect and the location was great, only one problem was bouncing around my head. I really wanted it but how could I possibly afford it? I was told that finding the money is the easiest part so just get out there and book viewings. They said find a great deal and the money will follow. I laugh about this nowadays as this was very naive of me.

The reality of my financial situation is starting to set in as there is no way I can possible afford this property deposit, I would need at least £25,000 which to me at this point in my life was never going to happen, however, I did not want to miss this opportunity and so I just had to find the money, one way or another, do whatever it takes as I have always said.

I was eager to capitalise on this opportunity so I thanked Ian for his time, we exchanged numbers for future opportunities and I left. I took some time to carry out some further more in depth due diligence, which included visiting a few HMO letting agents in the area to get their feedback, and the good news was everything was starting to become very clear that this deal was a great investment property which would be ideal for a multi-let HMO with four bedrooms.

My due diligence suggested that the price was a little inflating, now this is to be expected as the property had just undergone an expensive refurbishment, however, the ceiling prices for properties in this street of this size, type and layout were £85,000, at least that's what the agent told me and the sold comparable told me.

My offer was £82,600, so I called and offered this over the phone to Ian, I explained why I offered a lower price than the asking price and showed examples of properties similar that had recently sold for this amount of money. Always be specific with your offers and explain them to the vendor so they can understand where your offer comes from and why it is what it is. Today, I've put in many offers and I've never paid an asking price, I've always been specific with the offer and backed the lower offer up with supporting evidence.

I left for my next viewing and waited eagerly for Ian to call me. The rest of the viewings that day proved to be a waste of time, so I decided to call it a day in Hull and head home. It was late afternoon, around 4 pm I got a call from Ian to inform me the vendor appreciated my offer and had rejected it as it was too low, but countered my offer with a nice round figure of £85,000, this was exactly as I expected and in all honesty that's where I wanted to be.

If I had offered £85,000 in the first place, I'm pretty sure the vendor would have come back and said no, but would take £87,500. You need to understand that this is part of the negotiation process; it's a bit of a game so have fun…This is the property game, learn how to negotiate and play to win.

However, even at the lower price of £85,000, I still couldn't raise the finance for a deposit for the purchase. This is such a frustrating situation to be in. I've got this great deal, however, I cannot do anything with it because I can't raise finance for it. I'm sure you can all relate to this situation, however, I was determined not to give up on this deal, so I started speaking to other students from the training to see if they could help with the finance. I asked the few people I had in my life that I knew had money if they wanted to do a joint venture with me, but all of them said it was too risky.

There is always deal sourcing, I could sell the lead to investors. Now this strategy is a great way for people with little money to still profit from property, much like an estate agent, you get paid consultation fees by finding great deals for investors and I was learning how to do this from a training program I had recently been watching by an American mentor online, over the pond they call it property wholesaling, in the UK we call it property sourcing.

However, I did not have any connections or investors at this point to sell my deals to and very few people I knew who were able to offer any real help or advise, at the time I was working with another property investor who was running a property sourcing business and I approached him to see if he could offer any support, thankfully he did offer some support and offered to help me sell the deal to one of his investors that he had on a list of clients looking for deals.

I had to wait until my offer on the property was confirmed via email before we could offer it out to his investors list. Once we got that email confirming the property was secured we drafted an email and sent it out to the investors, and to my surprise, within the hour of the email being sent we had several investors saying they wanted more information about the deal.

We provided the further information over the phone and within a matter of hours we had the consultation fee paid into the bank account from an investor wanting to proceed with the deal. This blew my mind. I sold my first property deal to an investor who hadn't seen the deal, yet they were happy to pay me a fee upfront based on the due diligence we had provided.

The investor was a corporate manager called Chris, he worked in London for a large insurance company and he lacked time and knowledge to find suitable investment deals, so for Chris, a property being sourced for him is the ideal perfect solution as it gets him a deal without having to put much effort in at all. Chris actually became a very good investor of mine and I've since provided him with multiple property deals, he is extremely happy with the deals we have delivered for him and I'm now his personal bespoke property sourcer. I know what he wants and he trusts me to find the right deals for him and in return he is happy to pay me a finder's fee for this service.

Chris proceeded with the deal in Hull, he paid £2,700 plus vat as a consultation fee for our services in finding and negotiating the deal, and Chris was extremely happy with the find and the way I conducted the transition and property sale.

Sadly, although I wasn't in a position to purchase the first deal using my connection and knowledge I still managed to make a profit from the deal. This is what a smart entrepreneur does. This is why it is so important to get out there and just do it. On this deal I found a long-term investor with money to spend and furthermore, I gained valuable experience which would make the next property deal easier.

I didn't know at this point this would be the first of many property deals which would ultimately lead to me opening my very own property sourcing business where I deal directly with many wealthy investors. It amazes me just how many opportunities are out there if you're prepared just to take the plunge and get out there.

After my first deal, I then went on to find and pass on a deal a week for the next 9 weeks to investors. I got paid each time and learned many lessons in the process which I'll now share.

- Treat an estate agent as your best friend. They will be your best property sourcer if they like you. Do what you say you're going to do. Don't be late to appointments and always be straight with them. I get called a lot about off market deals from agents because of this. Bottles of wine and chocolates help too!
- Discipline your disappointment
- There's always a way to make it happen if you want to make it happen, just be creative. Although I couldn't buy this property, I still profited from the deal by thinking creatively
- Don't waste time on properties that clearly don't fit the criteria, you should be able to walk into a house very quickly and tell if it will work for you or not.

The first deal will always be the hardest, believe me the deals get easier as you do more. Think of it like driving, the first time you got behind the wheel you probably stalled the car and struggled, however, today if you are an experienced driver, it will be like second nature to you and this was exactly what happened to me, everything became much easier for me as I gained more practise and experience.

Before I knew it, I had successfully sold nine property deals in nine weeks to nine different investors whom I didn't know, so get this, in just nine weeks I found nine great property deals that investors were prepared to pay me a consultation fee for, and this was just the start of what was to come. Those nine weeks generated an income of £27,000. That's just crazy, literally this is the average salary in the UK and I just found a way to make this sort of money much faster.

If you're reading the book because you want to get involved in property sourcing then please get educated and just go for it but do it right and with integrity, make sure you check out our Property Sourcing Intensive online training for this strategy, this will give you a toolkit to get started.

One of the best things about property sourcing is that you are actively looking for properties and in this way you will always be "in the game". This way you will be meeting vendors and agents and you will come across many deals you will take on yourself. You will also be able to negotiate directly with vendors and you may well come across opportunities such as lease options and rent to rent deals along the way.

I've had the honour of training many people the right way to do property sourcing and I can tell you that the difference between the successful and those who give up are a key few elements. Those who succeed are driven, consistent and view a large quantity of properties. They never quit even when deals are not selling, even when they're having to give a refund or simply the market stock is low. They simply keep going.

If you would like to attend our free event The Property Accelerator you're welcome to come along and learn the exact steps to take, just visit www.alasdair-cunningham.com. I believe this strategy is essential for everyone wanting to make money from property. Think about it, you'll always be building your network of agents and investors. The best deals you find you can choose to keep for yourself or if you cannot for any reason then you have the skill set and network to still make a profit from the deal, and this is why everyone should at least learn the skills of property sourcing.

The greatest benefit from property sourcing is that you get the pick of the bunch of deals and that's how I found and secured my first property deal which I took on myself, and here's how I did that.

Chapter 7

Securing My First HMO

Putting yourself in the game even if you may not necessarily be ready to play is essential in my opinion, so many experiences and opportunities will come your way. This is exactly how I came across my first rental property which I managed to negotiate and secure using a very creative strategy called a lease option agreement, and it's all because I was out viewing properties for potential deals for investors.

At the time I was still working as a contractor, a job which involved me carrying out surveys of kitchens in the premises of every Dunelm Mill Home stores, showcase cinemas and other commercial kitchen outlets around the UK which meant I was travelling the country in order to carry out surveys of the kitchens. This was great because I was driving around the country in all different areas and was able to tie in property viewings whilst carrying out work for the company.

I committed to working for the kitchen company a few days a week which was great, they didn't mind when I was working for them as long as the contract that I'd committed to completed on time. This meant that I was left pretty much alone to get on with what I had to do.

During the week whilst I was in hotels, and in between sites I would be scraping the online sites for potential viewings and I started putting together a list of those suitable. I would then carry out as much due diligence prior to booking viewings as I could to prevent wasting time.

I'd realised that in previous weeks I had been wasting an awful lot of time by viewing properties that quite frankly weren't worth my time which I would have known if I had done a little more due diligence prior to viewing. I needed to start working smarter and become more productive.

During my searches I found a three bedroom terraced property which had two reception rooms. This property was in HU3 area of Hull which is just outside of the city centre, this property was ideal for a small 4 bed HMO conversion.

I made the appointments and attended the viewing. Now the agent here was actually really helpful and told me the whole background of the property, the owners were London based and have not had the best experience being landlords in Hull and had reached that point where they had just had enough.

The condition of the property was average at best, a light refurb was needed as although it was structurally sound with no real work needing doing it had become tired and run down.

Basically, new carpets, hard flooring in the kitchens and bathrooms, paint and decoration and installation of a partition wall for the extra bedroom were required so overall the works required wouldn't be that much, estimations were around £5000 for the works required.

I assessed the property along with carrying out extensive due diligence on the area for demand and values and I could see the potential of this deal so I decided to put forward an offer to the estate agent.

Currently, I was still not in a financial position to be able to finance buying the deal for myself, so my plan was to pass this onto an investor for a finder's fee. The owners were asking £88,500 for the property, however, after my research I felt that this price was a little high as I believed the true value was closer to £80,000, the street had sold comparable ranging from £78,000 - £90,0000, my offer of

£80,750 was put forward and surprisingly was accepted within the hour.

During my conversations with the agent, they let slip the vendor's position on the property; basically, the vendors were a couple from the south of England who purchased the property in 2007 for £96,500. The problem was they purchased the property the year before the credit crunch mortgage crash in Q3 of 2008, which acted as the catalyst for the biggest recession in modern times. Obviously, property prices had crashed across much of the country and indeed there are many locations that have still not recovered in value since the crash.

They were amateur landlords and thought the whole property market was easy. Unfortunately for them they made a number of mistakes as landlords including trying to self manage from a distance, which meant that no one was checking in on their asset. Actually they hadn't seen the asset for many years.

As of the day of viewing the property was vacant for eight months and the impression I got was the landlords had no intention of finding tenants, they were choosing to leave their property vacant instead of risking further issues, they'd previously had to replace the kitchen due to tenant damage and listening to the agent I could tell they'd had enough of this property. It was becoming a headache for them and they just wanted it out of their life.

With my offer being accepted I now needed to find an investor to take the deal so I hit the phones to touch base with previous investors and those I'd met at networking events. Within 24 hours I had an investor ready to proceed with the deal and his finders fee had been paid.

Now all we have to do is proceed to solicitor and let them do the searches and conveyancing so the exchange and completion date can be arranged, however a few weeks later I called the investor to check up on things and ensure everything was proceeding ok and he informed me that the vendors had to withdraw from the sale.

This was a shock to me as I knew the problems they were facing and I was surprised to say the least. They purchased the property in 2007, and during this time it was very possible to acquire a mortgage loan to value rates of 100% and in some cases 120% of the property value. Turns out they had highly leveraged the purchase using Northern Rock to finance the deal and their loan to value rate was ridiculously high meaning they were actually in negative equity, meaning they owe more on the lending than the property is worth.

In a nutshell the vendors would need to pay the difference between the sale price and the cost of paying off the mortgage which meant they would need to pay an additional £12,000 upon completion to the lenders to pay off the mortgage shortfall. They couldn't afford to do this, so we're left with no choice but to pull out of the sale.

I've been taught *"to discipline your disappointment"*.

This is easier said than done. Trust me, I've now got no property and a disappointed investor. My main concern here is that I didn't ruin my relationship with the investor, communication is key when things go wrong.

During the call we discussed options and alternatives as well as a refund for the finder's fee, which he declined instead he opted for a replacement property. I agreed to find a suitable replacement within four weeks and agreed that if I couldn't I would just refund him. This communication and proactive approach satisfied the investor that I was a person to trust and someone he wanted to work with. Transparency and honesty are incredibly important in this business.

Within a matter of weeks we had found another property, which he subsequently purchased and was very happy with. Now my Investor is happy, that's really all that matters.

A few days later I decided to try again with the original property as it was still being advertised online as I knew I could help the vendors get out of this position of negative equity. I had many creative strategies that I could use to help them.

I knew if I could talk directly with the vendors then I could definitely help them however getting the vendors details was never going to be straightforward as the agents are not allowed to disclose this information, so I started using various online search tools such a Land Insight and land registry to try and identify the property owners and hopefully somewhere is a residential contact address for them.

This search was proving not very useful however, I did manage to come across an old property rental listing on an online rental site, albeit it was from a few years ago, so I wasn't holding much hope of the contact box working, no harm in trying so I sent a message through the website not really holding out for any response.

Several weeks later, an email landed in my inbox from the owners sending me their contact information and asking me to contact them. I used this call to try and further understand the vendor's situation. Richard and Sue were both in corporate jobs in London and bought this property to invest some savings. They chose Hull because of the low cost of housing in comparison to London, however, they didn't really do any homework on the area or the types of tenants that they would be housing. They also had, in my opinion, a lacklustre approach to business and getting things done. It appeared that everything with them took forever to get done.

Before we could get to the creative strategies I wanted to ensure I was helping them as best I could, so to start with I was keen to introduce them to a local agent I had built up a relationship with to see if they could take care of the management of the property. I knew the area well and knew that with the right management team the property could be a great asset for them with little or no hassle.

The problem was that the vendors had become very much put off renting the property out, they had too many concerns, fears, and past trauma from previous tenants and simply had decided they wanted out of the property entirely. Owning a buy to let property had been a dream they had several years ago, however, for them this property was fast becoming a bit of a nightmare.

I did however manage to persuade them to speak with the letting agent but even after having the letting agent go out and appraise the property, provide them feedback on rental demand and prices, the vendors decided that they were still not keen to be landlords again. They were set to selling it and nothing was changing their minds.

The problem was that the property was not worth the value of their mortgage, and so they were now in a position of negative equity. Even if I could buy the property in the conventional way they were not able to cover the shortfall so unless I was to pay over the market value and help them out then quite simply a conventional purchase at a fair market value will never work.

We had the property valued by a local RICS approved surveyor and the valuation as expected was lower than their mortgage. This process was simple and effective because it was official, the property was not valued at what they think it is and it's now backed up by

RICS. This made my job of negotiating a deal easier and we have a clear black and white valuation report.

This report confirmed to the vendors that they were still in negative equity and they knew that they were not in a position to cover the financial shortfall. The negotiations were starting to reach a little stalemate as they were unable to take the lower offer and they also didn't want to let the property out, so what should I do

I decided to introduce them to another estate agent that I knew that was managing to sell their property stock fairly quickly. The agent has connections with some overseas buyers who were looking to invest in Hull and they were literally buying anything that was a viable rental investment, so the agency listed their property and communications between myself and the vendors pretty much dried up.

Now, I could have been disappointed that I never got the deal for myself but at the current time the deal wasn't there to be done. As for a deal to be made the situation must be a positive solution for both parties and they weren't prepared to budge on the price or in a position to settle the outstanding finance.

I was keeping my eyes on the property every time I was looking around the area and I noticed again that the property remained unsold after another month. There have been a few viewings on the property however, there are no offers that they can accept.

As you can imagine the vendors now are really at that point where a lot of time has passed, they've had to continue to pay the mortgage payments and they have no rental income and this whole situation is stressing them out. I had built up a good relationship with the vendors and we were chatting about alternative methods of purchase. It's worth noting that these alternative methods of purchasing are not right for everyone and only work in the right situation on the right property.

The agreement means that I would take control of the property straight away with the option to purchase for an agreed price at a later date. Legally they will still own the property, however, I would control the property. This is the basis of a *lease option agreement*.

In this agreement, I would essentially lease the property paying a monthly agreed lease payments, my responsibilities were that I would take care of the property and then I could rent the property out to tenants. Now in theory I imagine you're thinking well why can you make money but the vendors couldn't? Well, that's because I was prepared to rent the property as a house of multiple occupancy commonly known as a HMO. This would then increase the rent considerably, meaning I could take care of the property and still make a nice profit monthly from the deal.

After the period of time elapses as set out in the original agreement I would then have the option to complete on the purchase, once the housing market had had time to recover, done correctly and everyone makes money including the vendor.

As I said this type of arrangement is not for everyone, however, the vendors will make more money since they will be paid a monthly lease and at the end of the term will receive the selling price that they wanted. The property would also be looked after so they would not have to worry about this anymore. The vendor's mortgage would be paid by me allowing them to move on with their lives.

I discussed this type of arrangement with them briefly over the phone detailing what I could offer and how the agreement could work.

I asked them to go away and think about it and if they wanted further help and advice to contact my solicitor who would be handling the agreement. It's important that there is never a conflict of interest here and you must insist that the vendors are legally represented.

After our initial call I sent them an email with my outline proposal and details of two solicitors I knew could draft this type of agreement. I asked them to give the solicitors a call to discuss the legalities and ask any questions they may have. It is important to understand that the solicitor is instructed to represent the vendor and not you. They will correctly advise the vendor as their client for their best interests and are there to act as independent legal advisors. They are not there to sell or try and get the vendors to take your offer.

A week or so later I made contact with the vendors to check in and see if they had taken legal advice. They had and were keen to meet me to discuss the deal in person, which I was more than happy to do. Property, like any other business is ultimately about people and if you cannot trust or don't particularly like the person then it's unlikely a business deal will ever happen.

This meeting was primarily to get to know each other, since all our conversations had previously taken place over the phone. We had been speaking for several months by now but never actually met face to face, so we made arrangements for this meeting to take place.

We met and after the usual politeness we very quickly got down to business. Their main concern was what could go wrong and what if I didn't honour my agreement? After a while we ironed out all the questions and we started talking numbers and terms for the agreement. After a few hours we had reached an agreement in principle and here's what we left that day shaking hands on;

Purchase price in 5 years: £90,500 (their outstanding mortgage).

Monthly payment: £400

Their mortgage payments were £195 per month; we agreed to pay them an additional amount per month (extra £205 per month). The total lease payment to them, would therefore over the 5 years total £12,300.

In total, they will therefore receive:

- £90,500 (Purchase price in 5 years)
- £12,300 payment in rent which would be being paid off the mortgage each month which gives a total income £102,800

We put this into a heads of terms and sent this to my solicitor to draft the legal agreement. It's worth bearing in mind that essentially you're buying a house and this means that the conveyancing still has to take place so don't expect a quick turnaround, usual time frames are 6-12 weeks.

A couple of months later we completed the paperwork and the property was now in my company name and I could collect the keys. Finally I've got my first property deal and honestly I'm feeling very chuffed with myself, particularly because so far all I've paid is legal fees.

To convert the property into a small HMO I needed to carry out some works which cost just under £5,000. The works included

- Six fire doors throughout, including frames
- Fire alarm system, integrated
- Painting and decoration throughout
- New partition to split large open plan front room up to allow for a fourth bedroom
- Damp course treatment prior to decoration

- Repair to floor joists in hallway
- Tile kitchen and bathroom
- Install new shower

I managed to get all the work done for less than £5000 by pulling in favours and doing a lot of the work myself.

Currently, this property is fully tenanted making an income of £1,320 per month from four tenants. Three rooms are paying £350 per month and the single smaller room is let for £320 per month.

The property took just under three months to refurbish and was tenanted within a month of completion. Over the 5 year term, we will profit around £21,000 plus capital appreciation. I have a clause in the contract that says that I will pay the vendor a percentage of the uplift in value upon completion, to help them not feel hard done by when we complete.

Remember all these deals must be a win-win solution for both parties. The property is now tenanted, the landlord gets paid every month and I'm managing the property entirely.

I now have the option to buy the property for a fixed price of £90,500 in 2024. The property will in all likelihood have increased in value, which means I will also benefit from a percentage share of the capital appreciation. It is worth noting that the agreement I made with the vendor by which both the vendor and myself benefit from a shared percentage uplift from any capital appreciation, this was written into the contract.

Here are the figures:

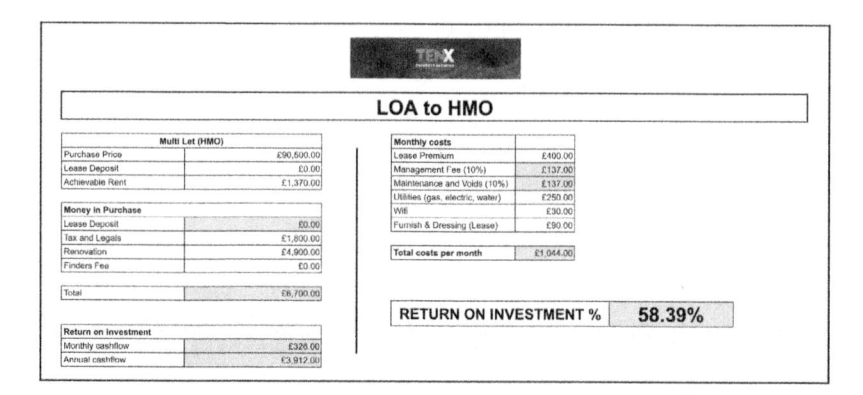

LOA to HMO

Multi Let (HMO)	
Purchase Price	£90,500.00
Lease Deposit	£0.00
Achievable Rent	£1,370.00

Money In Purchase	
Lease Deposit	£0.00
Tax and Legals	£1,800.00
Renovation	£4,900.00
Finders Fee	£0.00
Total	£6,700.00

Return on investment	
Monthly cashflow	£326.00
Annual cashflow	£3,912.00

Monthly costs	
Lease Premium	£400.00
Management Fee (10%)	£137.00
Maintenance and Voids (10%)	£137.00
Utilities (gas, electric, water)	£250.00
Wifi	£30.00
Furnish & Dressing (Lease)	£90.00
Total costs per month	£1,044.00

RETURN ON INVESTMENT %	**58.39%**

Whilst this type of investment is not for everyone they are however excellent when done correctly with the contract legal representation and contracts. It's very important to me and should be to you that all vendors should be treated with the utmost respect, dignity and care, since many of them will be in a highly stressed situation and we must ensure that they are fully represented and fully aware of what they are agreeing to.

Under no circumstances would I ever condone taking advantage of a vendor. It is imperative that these agreements are a win for all parties involved.

This particular property was proving to be a nightmare for the owners and they were in a terrible situation before I helped them. They owned a property which was in negative equity, had no buyers willing to pay the asking price they needed, had no interest in finding tenants and were losing money each and every month.

A lease option agreement has fortunately worked well for them, so much so that the vendors have since returned to me and asked me to do a similar deal with one of their properties in Croydon. Treat people fairly and they will always come back.

Key lessons about lease options:

- It must be win/win for both parties, do not take advantage of people using this method of acquiring property.
- Never give up. If I gave up when the deal fell through, I would never have got this deal
- Be open and honest at all times.
- Always offer help and advice before offering a LOA.
- Don't be greedy. If the equity increases drastically, I will share some of the uplift with them.

The property completed within 12 weeks, I then went to town sorting the property out and carrying out the required works to convert it into a 4-bedroom house of multiple occupancy.

I undertook a lot of the work myself and only used contractors where required to try to keep costs as low as possible. The refurbishment took 2 months to finish and once completed, the property was fully occupied in 8 weeks. I was a little surprised at how long it took to fill but the property proved to be a good deal.

I was actually becoming very good at building relationships with vendors and agents and was now starting to get approached directly about potential deals. This led me to start taking the deal sourcing element of my plans a lot more seriously as I needed to raise cash and I was good at finding deals.

I had no intention of slowing down so I decided it's about time that I started taking the whole property sourcing business a bit more seriously and I decided that now's the time to stop selling my deals through another sourcing business, where they take half the fee, but instead start my own business and keep all of the fee and in the next chapter I'll explain how I did exactly that. Keep reading.

Chapter 8

Your Money is in Your List

It was around April time I decided I wanted to deal directly with my own investors as previously I had been selling deals as a co-deal sourcer, however I had decided I now wanted to be running the business myself. I needed to get further training on certain aspects of the business, in areas such as compliance and the necessary legalities, so I took on some training to learn the exact steps I needed to take.

I quickly set about setting up the business and taking the required steps to become compliant. I had undertaken extensive research in the industry, looking at other companies and to my surprise found that most of the sector appeared very amateur. It seemed that there were lots of property sourcing companies out there that are passing deals to investors that simply do not stack up as deals, as well as many companies simply pulling deals from online property sites and trying to sell them without carrying out proper due diligence or stacking up the numbers.

The business of property sourcing falls under the estate agency act of 1979 which defines property sourcing companies as estate agencies. We as a property sourcing company therefore have to comply with this act. This requires the correct paperwork, legal compliances and structures to be put in place.

Many of the businesses you see trying to sell deals on social media quite simply do not comply with the regulations. If I was to use the services of a property sourcing business, then I would want to know that the people I am dealing with are compliant, honest, ethical and have good business practices in place.

I wanted to know that they are reputable and looking after me and my investment with the same care as they would with their own.

As an investor, the first thing you should be asking any property sourcing business you plan on working with is;

What redress scheme are you a member of and what is your membership number?

You should verify with the redress scheme that they are actually on the register, don't just take their word as gospel on this.

Here are the questions you should be asking all property sourcing companies before doing any business with them,

1) What property redress scheme do you belong to?

2) What is your property redress scheme membership number?

3) Who provides your insurance cover and how much does this cover? Ask to see the certificate.

4) Are they registered for data protection with the Information Commissioner's Office (ICO)?

5) What is their Anti Money Laundering license number?

You should be looking for the company presence online, and check all social media platforms, past client reviews, check for a consistent story of the company timeline such as, for instance;

Do they keep moving addresses?

Do they change names?

Do they have a registered address?

Are they easily contactable?

Check Companies' House for their company name and directors?

Also check that the owners have not been disqualified as directors on the companies' house website.

Reputable and compliant companies should also be asking you lots of questions as part of their compliance roles. Property sourcing companies have to carry out client due diligence, so please don't be offended if you are asked personal financial questions. You should actually be jumping for joy if they do this as it suggests they are doing their job correctly.

It was essential that for my property sourcing business to thrive and be a success then the first things that needed to happen were building good foundations.

This meant correctly setting the business, compliance and marketing up at the start. I know there are trainers out there that say forget the setup and just focus on making money and worry about compliance later but that rarely works in my opinion. Whilst I agree that making money is essential, setting a legal business up so you keep the money you've made is far more important.

How did I make £26,000 in the first 8 weeks of business?

Until now, I had been passing the deals that I found through another business as a co-deal sourcer and was receiving a percentage of the fee for these deals. This was okay to start with however, I was very aware that I was not actually building a business by doing this. I wanted to build my own investors database so I could sell directly. My investors list at this point was very small and consisted of people I'd met at various networking events along with those I have spoken to online through Facebook. It was a great start, but if I wanted to be successful, I needed to learn how to find investors. My current investors I had on the database were not actually buyers but more like people interested in what I was doing to try and learn. I wanted buyers with real money ready to spend.

One of the most important things you must understand is this;

*"**Your money is in your list.**"*

I now had the job of finding investors that wanted to join my investors list, but not just any type of investors. I wanted 'hot' investors that were actually looking to buy and could back up what they say with action. I wanted cash-rich, ready to buy, hot investors on my list.

Here's how I slowly but surely started to build a very active list which continues to grow and add between 40-60 new investors a week:

Step 1 – Tell The World what you do. Don't be ashamed or quiet about it. Ensure everyone knows what you're doing.

Step 2 – Build your online presence using Facebook, LinkedIn, Instagram and YouTube. Build the brand and market it, you need to market to the masses as loud as possible.

Step 3 – I record myself regularly and post to YouTube and Facebook, letting people know what I'm viewing and what deals might be coming up.

Step 4 – Have a website created to capture leads and keep investors up to date. You may have to give something away in exchange for details, for instance, I give away one of my basic Return On Investment (ROI) spreadsheets as a freebie.

Step 5 – Network, attend as many events as you can. Some of you will like this and others will hate this but get over it. Jump out of your comfort zone and just do it.

Step 6 – Immerse yourself in property, networking and business

Here is my 8 Step method I use for finding investors:

I	**Identify**
N	**Network**
V	**Value**
E	**Engage**
S	**Seminars**
T	**Tell**
O	**Online**
R	**Reputation**

Identify

Firstly, you need to identify the type of investor you are looking for. There is no point in doing any marketing until you know this, we're only aiming for wealthy cash-rich investors. So, we target the markets these individuals operate in and associate with. Think about it, most products that go to market are first underpinned by extensive market research to ensure the companies are targeting the correct demographic. One thing you need to identify is your market dominating position, this is the statement that defines your business and what your business does. Take a look at one of our statements that you can see on our website.

This clearly tells those visiting our website what we can offer them. Make sure you understand what it is your property sourcing actually offers your ideal client. Once you know this then you can network effectively.

Network

Once you know and understand who your ideal client is and what your Market Dominating Position (MDP) is then you can start looking for these clients. Make a list of where your ideal client is likely to be found. Once you have this list of where they're likely to be associating and networking then you must attend these places.

There is little point in trying to network if your target audience is not there, when you attend networking events you must have an agenda.

Why are you there?

What do you want to gain from attending?

Once you know this then you can prepare your introduction as most will allow delegates to offer an introduction of yourself. You should always take this opportunity. This is your opportunity to speak one to many and find your ideal client. Make the most of this opportunity.

Here's a typical 20 second introduction that I often use.

"Evening, my name is Alasdair and I specialise in matching up tired landlords looking to sell off some of their property with cash rich investors who are looking to buy right now. If you would like a free appraisal then let's chat in the break. Thank you".

This is how I would choose to introduce myself to landlords looking to sell their properties, it's quick, to the point and tells anyone in the room who is looking to sell property, that I can help them. This is by far the quickest way to tell your message to the whole room and that means you're more likely to find your ideal client.

I would alter the introduction depending on what my networking agenda was. You should prepare several 20 second pitches for different occasions depending on who you wish to network with, a couple of key points to remember here is this is your opportunity to come across professional and respectful so bear this in mind, make sure you're well presented, polite and listen to others when they speak. Stay off your phone!

It's very important that you do not sell or ask for finance during this pitch, you will be blacklisted and hardly anyone will come and see you. Don't be that person that is always there to take and never offer value or help others, remember networking is all about serving and building relationships. The quickest way to build relationships with other business owners is by adding value to them.

Value

This is a commonly used word and often people say they're adding value but in reality they're not. It's essential that you're always adding value to people before trying to sell to them and I mean genuine value that can help them in their business or life. What can you offer as a way to help others?

Maybe you can offer a free building survey, offer help in calculating the numbers of a deal for another attendee or maybe you're a builder and can offer a guide on how to assess properties. You can all offer value and all of you have a skill set that others may find useful. Your job is to present this in a useful manner in order to be remembered.

This approach builds credibility and trust and will help you build your database of potential buyers very quickly. It's essential you're not that person who is always selling something. You will quickly ruin your reputation and people will just pass you by.

Engage

If you take someone's details or have an investor join your list, then please ensure you engage with them. It's no good taking the details of an investor, ignoring them for 3 months and then randomly contacting them trying to sell. They will have forgotten about you and your business and they need to hear from you regularly.

Nobody builds a long-term relationship in one meeting and certainly no one hands over £1,000s in finder's fees to someone they have just met, you must enter the investors into a know like and trust campaign for your business, which is a series of emails that detail and keep engagement for your business. For example

Email 1 - Thank you for joining the database, you could then offer some details of what they can expect after joining your database.

Email 2 - Here's our compliance information - List all compliance details so they know you're trustworthy.

Email 3 - Testimonial email - Reviews and feedback from past customers.

Email 4 - I send details explaining how to reserve a deal from us once they receive the email.

Email 5 - Past deals - show and tell a past deal you've sold.

These emails build your business into their daily life and will mean they start to know you, like you and are starting to build trust in your business. I contact my investors every Tuesday at 9am without fail and for those investors that are on my VIP investors list they also receive an additional email on Monday at 2pm.

Seminars

I find many investors at seminars as you'll find many investors are always learning and growing as a person, so you'll often find good investors whilst you're attending seminars. You should become a bit of a networking ninja and try to meet as many people at these events as possible. Make the most of these events even if they're online zoom events. I mentored a lady who hated networking and I managed to persuade her to start networking. The reason was, she believed that her accent was hard to understand and this became a limiting factor in her business. Her business was suffering because she couldn't get over the thought of people not understanding her, when in fact her accent was perfect and nobody had an issue with it.

I managed to get her to attend online training events from her home country for people looking to learn about property investing. She started attending these training events and if she ever got the opportunity to speak she took it, very quickly the organisers could see she knew what she was talking about and with her connections in the UK she was soon invited as a guest speaker to present about the UK markets. This just shows you that when you put yourself out there amazing things happen.

When I attend any training event as a delegate I always have my Ipad with me and I always have my website open and ready, the reason being is when I'm chatting or (selling) to someone I can get them onto my database straight away. All too often at these events everyone swaps business cards but the reality is that most business cards end up in the bin where by if you take your tablet or laptop and get them on your database right there and then you will find and secure more potential investors.

It's imperative that you're well presented when you attend seminars, pay attention and do everything to the best of your ability. Remember everyone watches so be mindful if you're trying to attract people into your business that they are watching all the time, you want to make sure you're always acting how you want to be seen.

Tell

Tell The World what you're doing. Literally scream about it from the hill tops and don't stop. Use your social media profile to broadcast this by using videos, posts and creative artwork. It's amazing what happens when you tell the world what you are doing, the deals you are finding and the investors you are helping. You will get people messaging you asking for similar deals, offering joint venture opportunities and business. Be loud and proud about what you do and your business.

Take a look at my new property networking instagram account alasdair_cunningham. Go ahead and follow this page and see what we post to let people know what we're doing.

Take the middle post "My students made a total of £565,000 since working with me".

What does that tell you? Would this post make you intrigued about what's going on? Would you want to be involved in that?

The answer is mostly yes, because of course it's a very informative post that is likely to create engagement and is all about me telling people what we are doing. Remember, Tell the World.

Online

Use online forums, social media and email marketing to add value and contribute to your potential audience. The more value you add, the more people will want to do business with you. It's that simple. We call it 'serving before you sell' and I suggest you become accustomed to this practice.

I only use online methods to direct people to my website where they can join my mailing list. I never sell a deal directly on any social media platform. Your strategy by contrast should be to build your list.

Remember at all times "your money is in your list" and everything you do should be with this in mind. Use your online presence to build your brand and position. Become known as a person of service.

Reputation

Reputation is critical if you are to be trusted. Always do what you say you are going to do. Be nice to everyone and be ethical and honest at all times. My father has always said that it takes years to build a good reputation but that it can be lost overnight.

Look after people and operate your business ethically and legally. This is the foundation of all long standing successful businesses.

You may encounter business problems, unhappy customers and complaints, but it is how you deal with these that will build your reputation. I have no issues with any of my investors because any problems that occur get dealt with quickly and correctly. I suggest you also do this.

Building a list of 'ready to buy' investors is not easy and can be very time consuming. It has taken me three years to build a list of just 9,629 investors, but this has been done entirely organically using the approaches I've described above.

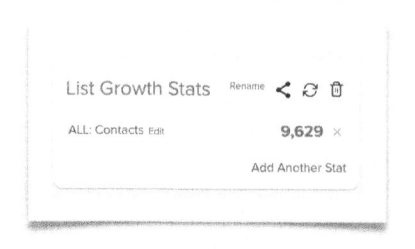

List Growth Stats	Rename		VIP Deal Alerts	Rename	
ALL: Contacts Edit	9,629 ×		VIP Deal Alert Member Edit	122 ×	
	Add Another Stat		PMT: via AC Stripe Edit	52 ×	
			PMT: via PayPal Edit	3 ×	
			PMT: OLD CherryPick Edit	67 ×	
				Add Another Stat	

I've also attracted over 122 VIP investors into my database which means these investors pay me £24.99 each month to receive the database the day before public release of my deals. Think about the statement "the money is in your list" I've created 122 x £24.99 = £3048.78 passively from my investors list each and every month or annually £36,585.36. This alone is a very healthy UK wage.

I've never to date paid for any advertising for my investors list, although I may choose to do so in the future, this is organic growth which is by far the best way. I've always trained my investors as well, this is a process which I'll teach you when you attend my Property Sourcing Intensive training. What this means is my investors are trained to open my email and act how I want them to act when I send an email.

Take a look at our open rates for emails, if you know anything about open rates you'll know that the standard open rate for a database is 2% - 5% which means most people on a database never open an email from a company. Think about it, how many unopened emails are currently in your inbox.

We're seeing an average open rate of 40% for all of our emails and that's why we can sell deals week after week.

Email	Status	Opens
Deals you don't want to miss out on! Sent Jun 28th at 3:52 AM	Sent	35.9%
£565,000 in CASH since Jan 2022! ... Sent Jun 27th at 5:55 PM	Sent	24.7%
BTL offering high returns!! Sent Jun 27th at 9:06 AM	Sent	40.1%
Rent to SA deals!! Sent Jun 24th at 4:03 AM	Sent	37.7%
Rent to SA ready to be secured! Sent Jun 23rd at 4:59 AM	Sent	37.7%
£111,000 in 6 months! Sent Jun 22nd at 10:33 AM	Sent	40.3%
New deals ready to be secured! Edited on Jun 21st at 5:26 pm	Draft	-
Mid Week R2SA Deal Sent Jun 22nd at 4:02 AM	Sent	25.2%
New deals ready to be secured! Sent Jun 21st at 3:57 AM	Sent	38.4%

You are going to need a website to direct people to and you can do this very cheaply. I used www.wix.com for my original website which I had created for £199 and then undertook a little editing to make it mine. I originally had this hosted on 123.reg.com for £9.99 per month from memory. Within the website, I included an opt in form to join my mailing list which was facilitated by www.allclients.com. Once this is set up, the whole thing is automated.

I've since changed my website and customer relationship manager (CRM) system to cope with greater volumes of business, but I would start simply as I did, since this will help keep start-up capital low and will work perfectly well at the start. I would suggest you try to make it as simple as possible for an investor to join your database.

Chapter 9

Property Sourcing Business Setup

Now that I was slowly building a database of investors, the next step was to become compliant before I could introduce an investor to a property deal.

I had to research exactly what was required and have created a seven step system to help others start a successful property sourcing business.

S	Setup / Legalities
O	Offer
U	Understanding
R	Research
C	Clients
E	Exchange
R	Reputation
S	Systemise

Setup / Legalities

You must set your business up correctly. Since you will be trading as an estate agency, your business will fall under the estate agency act of 1979. You will need;

- A Ltd Company (you can operate as a sole trader but this is not advisable)
- To be a registered member of a property redress scheme; there are currently two schemes available as of 2022; these

are the Property Ombudsman and the Property Redress Scheme.

- Insurance
- Data Protection License
- Anti-money Laundering Registration
- Website
- Marketing
- Legal Paperwork

I will cover the compliance in greater detail further on in the book; the above is just an overview.

Offering

You must learn how to offer your deals to your investors list. When we offer a deal, we have investors waiting to see them and our deals are typically reserved within an hour. Mastering how you offer your deals will make your business a whole lot easier. We train our investors to work my way. It's my business and if they want to use our services then they work to my systems and methods; in a nutshell we have rules we stick to whether the investor is buying their first deal or their fifth.

The rules are the same for all. My business - my rules.

Understanding

You need to understand what your investors are looking for. There is no point offering HMOs to investors only interested in Below Market Value deals. Having a clear understanding of your market and investors' needs, means you can market to them far more efficiently. I found it easiest to understand what your investors are looking for when they first join your list. If you join my list, you will see how I do this; we simply have a drop-down menu with all the different strategies and types of deals we can provide. Think about it, if you opened a shop would you really offer products no one wants to buy? Of course not. So why would you look for property deals that your investors cannot afford. Set your business up and become a specialist "HMO Property Sourcer" as opposed to a "I'll source anything type of company". You must understand your ideal client's needs.

Research

You need to understand how to research and carry out due diligence on your investors and properties.

Does the deal stack up?

Would you buy it?

Do the numbers work?

I tell all my staff to only ever sell a deal for a finder's fee if they would personally buy the deal with their own hard earned money. If they wouldn't part with their hard earned money on the deal, then quite simply it's not a deal we would sell.

Clients

Without these you will never make any money from your hard work. Master finding these and you will be able to pick and choose your clients. The money is in your list and you need a large, qualified client list who are looking to invest in deals and opportunities. I have been able to raise finance from my list for deals I have bought from my investors list, your list of clients are there for you to build your business with and that means you can utilise this list of clients for property sourcing, raising finance, joint venture and business partnerships. You've built your list so you must capitalise on these ideal clients.

Exchange

You need to be able to exchange to get paid and for this you will need contracts and paperwork in place to enable this. You must ensure you have the right paper in place to ensure that you're not breaking the law, breaching AML regulations and importantly not getting cut out of the deals.

When you purchase the Property Sourcing Intensive online training you get, as a gift from me, the contract package that we use in our property sourcing business, alternatively you could find a solicitor to draft you a template contract that you can use and you'll pay a couple of thousand pounds. My contract package from my solicitors cost my business over £4,000.

Reputation

Reputation is critical if you are to be trusted. Always do what you say you are going to do. Be nice to everyone and be ethical and honest at all times. Your business must trade in a compliant and ethical manner at all times. You as the director of the company have a legal obligation to ensure your complying with company law, the estate agency act and good business practices.

You'll also need to have systems in place for a complaints procedure, again you can access ours when you take on the property sourcing intensive training program.

Systemise

You need to systemise the business as far as possible. Have systems in place to take care of less important roles such as Customer

Relationship Management (CRM) systems for client interactions, virtual assistants to take calls, to do paperwork, for finding leads, addresses etc.

Here's a few tips to systemise your business. Write down all the tasks in your business that need to be done every day so that you still make money.

Value each task 1-10

Now assign a value to yourself, for me I'm a 10 which means if I haven't assigned a 10 to the task then I don't do it. I only undertake tasks assigned a 10, every other task can be outsourced to others.

At the start you'll be a much lower number but I suggest you learn to fire yourself as quick as possible from your business if you want a business otherwise you've just created yourself a job.

You can start outsourcing very cheaply using websites such as fiver, people per hour and freelancer. There are many ways to outsource and systemise your business and you can start this from as little as $2 an hour.

Remember a business should be a systemised machine that makes money while you're doing what you choose to do, however, as with all businesses you're going to have to put the hard work in at the start to get it making money. There will come a point when you must only be focusing on the income generating tasks and not the mundane admin tasks.

Whenever I teach my students through the Property Sourcing Intensive, I focus a lot on treating your property sourcing company as a business and not a side hustle, this is a real life business that done right can make you literally hundreds of thousands of pounds a year. I'll prove everything I say as you get to the end of the book as I'm sure some of you wont believe this.

Chapter 10

Property Sourcing Compliance

Do it Right from the Start - Business Set up and Compliancy

Deal sourcing falls under the estate agency act of 1979; you can find the legislation here if you need clarification on this:

http://www.legislation.gov.uk/ukpga/1979/38

To comply with the act, you need to set your business up correctly from the start before you sell your first deal.*

Step 1: Set up and register your limited company

Having a limited company set up, ring-fences the company's liabilities within the company to protect you as an individual from being personally liable. I used a business formation company:

www.companiesmadesimple.com

You can set up your new limited company in less than 15 minutes with the costs ranging from £14.99 to £99.99. Each package includes different levels and services. I opted for the ultimate package as this included mail forwarding and a registered handling address from your home.

*Disclaimer: This is how I have set up my business after advice from my accountant and legal professionals. Please satisfy yourself that the following is appropriate to your personal situation. Please seek advice from a legal professional and accountant.

This is important - since it is not advisable to have your home address as the registered address

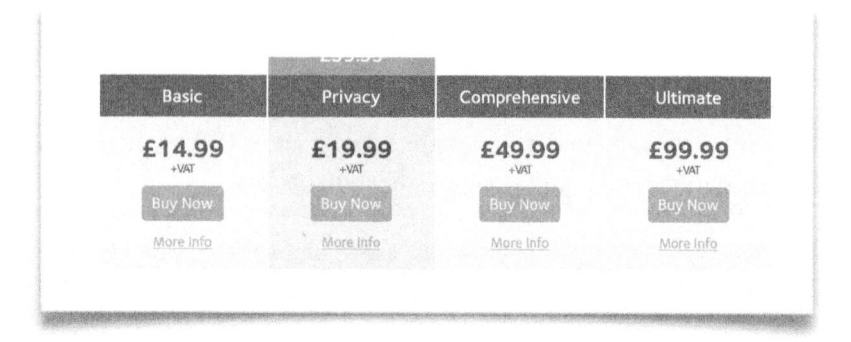

Basic	Privacy	Comprehensive	Ultimate
£14.99 +VAT	£19.99 +VAT	£49.99 +VAT	£99.99 +VAT
Buy Now	Buy Now	Buy Now	Buy Now
More Info	More Info	More Info	More Info

You can opt to use your accountant to set up your limited company, however, it is fairly straightforward to do and much cheaper if you do it yourself.

You will need to use SIC code 68310 when registering your company.

I wouldn't try to kill two birds with one stone either; let's say you have a rent to rent business and you wanted both your rent to rent business and your property sourcing business all under the same business.

I'd recommend each strategy has its own Ltd company set up with their own bank accounts and insurance cover etc.

This was the advice I was given by my accountant at the time.

You should refer to your accountant for the latest up to date information and advice on this, since the most appropriate approach will depend a lot on your personal circumstances.

Step 2 - Bank Accounts

You will need a business bank account. You will find all high street banks offer business accounts. You can open an account online fairly easily. I currently use Nat-West bank who have been absolutely fine.

When you are opening your account, you will require a client account. A client account is an individual account that is used to hold funds which currently do not belong to the business, such as for instance if you're holding a deposit for a property on behalf of the client. This money does not belong to the business and therefore should not be used by the business or be included in the business accounting.

Client accounts have protection which means if the business goes into administration, then the clients' account money is protected. In some circumstances you will not require a client account. I would take advice from the bank and your solicitor as to whether the way you operate your business means you legally require a client account or not.

Step 3 - Insurances

You MUST be fully insured to trade legally and you will need the following cover:

a) Professional Indemnity Insurance

Minimum cover required £100,000 to cover you for any advice which you give to an investor in a professional capacity; this insurance will also cover you for a breach of professional duty in business dealings you undertake in exchange for a fee. Please ensure you take out a suitable level of insurance to fully cover any business dealings you undertake.

b) Vehicle Insurance

If you are using a vehicle to assist with viewings then you will need to have business insurance in place. It's worth keeping a vehicle record to monitor when you use the vehicle for business mileage. You may be able to just add business usage to your current insurance policy.

c) Employers Liability Insurance

If applicable, you will need an employer's liability policy to cover for any accidents, injuries or illness as a result of the employer's work.

My brokerage firm is: Duncan Clark Insurance Brokers, and my broker is Richard O'Neill.

01727 852299

piinsurance@dcib.co.uk

They offer a tailored Insurance package for Property Sourcing Companies.

Step 4 - You must be a registered member of a property redress scheme

There are currently two scheme's which facilitate the estate agency business and they are;

The Property Ombudsman

www.tpos.co.uk

The Property Redress Scheme

www.theprs.co.uk

You only have to register for one of these schemes.

Each of the redress schemes has their own individual guidelines and practices that you must adhere to so simply registering and then forgetting about it is not good enough.

You need to know how each redress scheme expects you to conduct your business and trade accordingly. It's your responsibility to ensure you are in compliance with your chosen providers terms and conditions and code of conduct.

Step 5 - Register your company for a Data Protection License

www.ico.org.uk

You are required to register your company for a data protection license. As you will be handling client's personal data and paperwork, your company must be registered. You must also ensure you handle all customer data privately and securely. The cost for this is £40.

GDPR - General Data Protection Regulation

There are lots of practical tips / sites available to ensure you comply with GDPR. Please ensure you read up on this and ensure you stay within the law.

A good book for advice is "GDPR for Dummies"

In summary you need permission to contact people via email, if you use a well-known CRM platform such as All clients or mail chimp then they will keep you on track.

As a general rule you're responsible for handling your clients information responsibly and that means you have to have a process in place to ensure their data is protected.

Always use secure company email addresses, never share their information with anyone outside your organisation and treat their personal data as you would want yours treated.

Step 6 - Anti-Money Laundering License

Depending on how you operate your business depends on how you handle the payments, we only ever charge a consultation or finder's fee for the lead to the property deal. At no time will we ever handle or hold the investors monies for the purchase of the deal, or in fact any part payment or deposit which will be paid towards the deal.

This being said, we still need to comply with Anti-Money-Laundering (AML) regulations as we are involved in the transaction.

Property is the number one vehicle used to launder money and the government is really starting to crack down and enforce action against those who breach the guidelines for AML checks.

Please check the HMRC website for advice on staying compliant and learn how to keep track and monitor all your financial dealings to comply with anti-money laundering registration.

You can find out how to get registered below. You will need your UTR (Unique Tax Reference) number for your Ltd company to get registered.

https://www.gov.uk/anti-money-laundering-registration

Here's a brief overview of what you will be required to check;

- Proof of identity (valid photographic ID, verified by a professional body such as solicitor or postmaster).
- Proof of address (valid utility bill such as council tax or bank statement, verified by a professional body such as solicitor or postmaster).
- Proof of funding (bank statement or screen shot).
- Source of funding (for the full amount of monies required, this could be bank statements, SA302, accounts, proof or inheritance, mortgage offer etc.

It's called know your customer (KYC) and you must do this if you undertake any business dealings with an investor.

Here's further information if you wish to read up more on it:

https://www.gov.uk/guidance/money-laundering-regulations-your-responsibilities

This is a legal requirement: If the client does not comply with any of your KYC requests then simply walk away from the deal. We out-sourced all our compliance obligations to ensure we are always compliant.

On the Property Sourcing Intensive online training we cover compliance and AML in detail, make sure you're getting access to this training to stay on top of the game.

Costs to becoming compliant (April 2018):

Property Sourcing Compliance Start Up Costs.	
Set Up Limited Company	39.99
Insurance - Duncan Clark Insurance services	350
Insurance - Vehicle Business Cover added on to my personal insurance policy - I keep a mileage record	180
Property Redress - The Property Ombudsman Scheme	294
Data Protection License www.ico.org.uk	40
Anti-Money Laundering License	240
Total Start Up Costs to become Compliant	1143.99

People often ask me if they can co-deal source to get them started. Co-deal sourcing is a great way to start and get experience. This means you provide the deals to the compliant business who should then carry out their own due diligence on the deal and then if suitable they can offer the deal to one of their investors.

The compliant business would handle all aspects of the transaction with the investor and you as the co-deal sourcer would not be involved in the process. You are not required to be compliant to co-deal source as you are not dealing with the investor, finance or paperwork for any legal matters.

To complete the compliance side of the business you will also need various documentation, procedures and policies in place - all of which need to be documented.

We provide examples of all these documents to anyone who comes along to our advanced training Property Sourcing Intensive.

Chapter 11

A Years Salary in just two months

I'm now fully compliant, set up and ready to start making some real money. Up until now I've been selling my property deals through another sourcing company so I arranged to spend a day with them to further expand my knowledge. I asked them if I could bring three deals, which I had viewed and undertaken due diligence for, for them to sell so that I could watch the process and learn. I agreed that whatever fee we took that day that they could keep all of it in exchange for spending a day with me.

We spent a few hours just going through some deals together to ensure they were good enough to sell before we drafted the sales email to send to his investors. The information on the sales email is fairly limited and we do this for a reason.

The reason for this is to keep the information limited in order for people to enquire through the correct contact point, basically we keep the information limited in order to get potential investors on the phone as we will have a better chance of selling the deal to them.

The email has been sent and within literally 30 minutes the text messages from investors started coming in, they were asking for a call back to discuss the deals.

I kid you not... within half an hour we had 25 text messages from investors from all over the world and once you see this, you'll never forget it.

We then called the investors back in the order they texted in and ran each person through the deal, gave them all the information and helped them come to a decision if they wanted to proceed or not.

There was no hard selling or pushy sales, just this is the deal,

What do you want to know?

How do you want to proceed?

Simple, it seemed anyway.

Within a few hours all three deals were sold and the full finder's fees had been paid to reserve them. Literally, in a morning, we had banked over £8,000 and I just couldn't not see this as a day that changed everything. When you see someone make £8000 in a matter of hours then you'll never have a job again. Annoyingly, this lesson cost me £8000 as I agreed that the team could have all of the sourcing fees for spending the day with me.

Never mind, let's take these lessons and get out there and find some more deals, this time I'm keeping the full finders fee for the next deals.

As I've been building my investors list over the last few months, I had a small handful of investors that had committed to taking a deal off me if I found what they wanted, so with this in mind I drafted an email outlining the deals I had and sent them to my list of potential investors.

I eagerly awaited some sort of response. An hour passed and nothing, then the morning had passed and still nothing, not one single text message.

My list currently had 77 investors on it so I knew deep down it would be a struggle to sell these deals to such a small list of investors but I kept trying. I was expecting the same sort of results as I saw the other day in the office. I honestly thought this was easy and I would send an email and ping I'd make £3000 the same day, however this was not to be the case. Nobody got in touch.

This led to my negativity and scepticism reappearing and I soon started to disbelieve again.

Was it really that simple?

Send an email and make all this money.

Come on, that's just not possible.

In my head I was now doubting the deals we sold yesterday. Did they really sell or were the investors that bought friends of the team just to make them look good, honestly I started to question everything I'd witnessed that day.

Was it all smoke and mirrors?

Now I could continue on this downward spiral however, that won't pay my bills and I don't quit easily. The thing is I'm not the first person to do this business, nor will I be the last and if they can do this, so the bloody hell can I.

I decided not to let my mind take me out of the game but to have a break, get away from the screens and phones and take my dogs for a walk.

On the walk, I went out to the fields behind my house. It is a wide open area with streams and empty fields, where the dogs can have a run around and I can just chill out for a little while.

As I always do, I put headphones in and watched a video on YouTube by Arnold Schwarzenegger talking about his journey to becoming the 'Terminator' . It's great, watch it when you get a minute.

The video that came on afterwards really resonated with me. This video got into my head and made me wake up a little, the video is saved in my playlist and I play this constantly especially if i'm feeling demotivated.

It can be found on YouTube as;

"Everyone dies, but not everyone lives"

Prince Ea.

Please watch this video, it will open your eyes and I hope to motivate you like it did me as whenever I'm feeling low, I replay this video.

So many of the words and lyrics resonate with me such as:

"Sometimes you got to leap and grow your wings on the way down."

This line has helped me make what should be hard decisions very easily. For instance, I was asked to speak on stage in front of 80 strangers by an event host who had followed my journey.

Every part of me was saying no way, I'm not ready for this.

I've never spoken in front of more than 20 people and even that was terrifying. I mean public speaking is ranked as more frightening than death by many. I am pleased to say that I decided to "leap and grow your wings on the way down" thanks to Prince EA.

I took the opportunity and it wasn't nearly as bad as I expected. I mean it was bad but not that bad!

If I took myself out of the game by saying no, I would never have had the opportunity to speak on the same stage as Armand Morin - a very successful US internet marketing guy.

Ten years earlier I had been studying his internet marketing online training course. I was a customer of his buying his products and now here I was sharing a stage with him.

How the heck did this happen?

It's very simple, I said YES! Even though I wanted to say no.

Thanks, Prince Ea. I owe you big time.

Back to selling my first deal to my own investors, I returned home from walking the dogs and checked my phone and saw a missed call, the call was from a guy called Adam.

I met him some weeks prior at a networking event in London, he was looking to invest into HMO deals. However, as this was going to be his first HMO, he had been advised that he would need landlord experience before a lender would lend for a HMO deal as they are more complex deals.

He was advised to buy a single let property first, so that was what he planned to do.

One of the deals I sent out was a 2-bed terraced property I had secured directly with the vendor as part of a probate sale. The family just wanted a quick sale with no hassle and we agreed a sale price of £57,000.

The property was run down and tired, needed a new kitchen, bathroom, and decoration throughout. In the same street, properties of the same structure and size were selling or recently sold for between £85,000 / £95,000.

I explained the deal, talked him through the layout, condition, refurbishment and market for the property. I explained we have a team ready to do the work and he could be completely 'hands-off' if that is what he preferred.

I explained why we charge a fee, how much we charged and told him all about our due diligence process and viewing process. I also reassured him of our terms and conditions and our refund policies.

I explained as per our terms, that he would have a period of time to carry out all his own due diligence and if he felt the deal wasn't for him, then he could simply request a refund and walk away. He was fine with this and he said he'd be in touch.

I had no other messages or interest in the email I sent out this week, so I tried to stay positive and I cracked on with my week of viewing properties which led to me Wolverhampton.

Throughout the day I kept an eye on my phone and noticed Adam had sent me a WhatsApp message, he had spoken to his broker, the finance was in place and he wanted to proceed. I was literally shaking in disbelief, could it be I've just sold my first deal to my very own investor.

I quickly jumped on a call with Adam and rightly so, he wanted to go ahead with the deal. I sent him the terms and conditions followed by the invoice. I eagerly awaited his payment to hit the account as I continued with my viewings that day, just a few hours later £3000 landed in my bank account! This was my first deal and I've been paid! They say that the deal hasn't sold until you've seen the gold. Well, now I've seen the gold.

I hand held Adam throughout the buying process and upon completion, I arranged for the build team to collect the keys and start the work. The work took six weeks to complete and Adam was able to refinance the property to a value of £90,000

This meant at a loan to value rate of 75% Adam was able to pull out £67,500 which meant after all costs he had less than £4,000 of his own money left in the deal.

He was very happy with the deal and our services as we managed the deal from start to finish including introduction to letting agents.

This was the first of nine deals I passed on in 9 weeks which in total generated an income of £27,000. A yearly salary for a large portion of people in the UK.

Today I have a healthy investors list of nearly 10,000. We have no trouble selling deals and have many happy investors who simply buy from us because they don't have the time nor the inclination to find deals themselves.

At time of writing this June 2022, we've packaged and sold over 440 property deals and I've systemised the business in order to allow it to scale. This frees up my time in order for me to develop and grow other businesses including my training business where I have created a program all about property sourcing called "Property Sourcing Intensive"

This is by far the most affordable, valuable and comprehensive training package in the UK. Check out website for more information and take advantage of this today

www.alasdair-cunningham.com

- Compliance
- Setup
- Finding and analysing deals
- Sales

- Finding Investors
- Client due diligence and AML
- CRM, website and marketing
- Legalities of sale
- Aftercare
- Systemisation

This training is not for everyone as it requires a lot of hard work and effort to be successful, but when you get there, the results are worth all the effort; this certainly is not an overnight success type of business.

You will need a lot of hard work, persistence and a heap load of implementation to make it in this business, but if you realise this we can certainly help you.

Chapter 12

Property Number Two In The Bag

As I was slowly building a bank balance from my sourcing business, I was in saving mode. I wanted to create a healthy bank account so I was only really looking for deals that I could acquire using creative strategies, such as rent to rent, lease options or delayed completions.

Now let's be straight from the offset, you don't actually own anything using these strategies until you complete on the deal, but you can certainly benefit from cash-flow when done right.

I had found a property advertised on gumtree for a four-bedroom city centre property in Wolverhampton; the property was being advertised as a single let property and available from July after the university had finished for the year. I arranged to view this property as I made some initial interesting observations during the initial due diligence.

In the photographs on Gumtree, I could clearly see the doors had door closers on them; now in my mind not many single let properties have fire doors fitted and this got me thinking that the property at some point may have been converted into being a HMO.

I attended the viewing and met the owner, Steve, a landlord of 18 years who owned a portfolio of multiple properties and was now looking to retire from property and live a quiet life in the country somewhere.

Steve had owned this property since 1999 and had operated it as a single let mainly for many years. As the university expanded, he then converted it into an HMO and rented this to students. However, Steve was not charging anywhere near the right amount for the rooms.

He was letting the property to one tenant but with permission for them to allow friends to live there as well. Basically, it was being run as an HMO but earning single let money. From memory Steve was achieving £550 rental income per month.

Now, I knew in the area you could achieve £320 - £400 per room per month in the WV1 postcode area. The thing is that Steve was a nice landlord, he cared about his tenants and didn't want to charge them the going rate. He was happy with £550 per month. As he said, everyone's happy, the rent gets paid, so why rock the boat.

Great advice from a seasoned landlord.

Steve showed me around and we chatted about property and his business and other properties he had - along with his plans for retirement. Steve is late 60's and wants to retire in 4-5 years and move to his holiday home in France. He was planning on selling his properties closer to retirement.

This got me thinking about my proposal, originally, he was planning on trying to offer a rent to rent type deal, however a lease option could be far better and actually more suitable for Steve.

We discussed using a lease option agreement instead of a rent to rent model; this would mean I would lease the property now and then complete the purchase in 5 years when he would be looking to sell it anyway. For Steve this would be a good deal - providing we could agree on the numbers.

I agreed in principle with Steve to pay a fixed amount each month as a lease premium, in this case £500 per month. I would take care of all of the maintenance and I would have the option to purchase the property for £130,000 in 5 years. In the meantime, I would benefit from the profit in cash flow and then the capital appreciation once the purchase was complete. Steve said to leave it with him and he'd be in touch. Of-course, I said that would be no problem but what I would do would be send over a breakdown of the offer via email and in the email, I'd put the contact information of our solicitor who could represent him throughout the transaction. If he had any questions, he could ask them and they would answer all the legal questions he might have.

I would not wish to answer legal questions about this agreement as this could be seen as unethical. I would want a completely independent solicitor who is not representing myself to answer Steve's questions. In this way he would be getting the best possible advice from a solicitor who would represent his interests.

A few weeks had passed and I hadn't heard from Steve so I put this down to experience. I said to myself 'what will be will be'. Another day another deal and I continued with searching for deals. I had several further viewings that week and was on the road when I got a text from Steve.

Steve had spoken with the solicitor and was happy with the legalities, was comfortable with me and would like to arrange a call to discuss the next steps. I arranged to call him back and run through the details with him. We arranged to meet up in a motorway service on the M6 to sort out the next steps.

I bought a copy of the head of terms with me, which is basically a document that lays out what we had agreed beforehand. We both signed this and I sent these to the solicitors so they could prepare the legal documentation. Three months later, the contracts were all complete and I arranged to collect the keys.

I carried out a range of works to the property to ensure that the property would get maximum income and provide a great home to four tenants.

The works included;

- Painting and decoration throughout
- New carpets through including vinyl flooring
- New kitchen / utility room tiling
- New taps throughout
- New back door

The work took 6 weeks and was done by myself and my father to save money. We carried out all the work to a very good standard for just under £4,000. I used the fact that I would be investing in the refurb to negotiate a no deposit deal with Steve. This was not a no money down deal, but I did use a credit card to pay for everything to acquire this deal. I then paid the credit card off with the profit from the rental income.

Here's the breakdown of costings for refurbishment:

- £1,200 - Carpets and Vinyl floor - local contractor
- £1000 - Paint throughout - local supplier and found a local tradesman who assisted for a few days for £75 per day
- £150 - Taps for kitchen and bathroom
- £550 - Back door
- £350 - Tiling
- £180 - New door handles / numbers
- £360 - Garden clearance front and back

Most of the work was carried out by myself and my father apart from the certification for the gas and electrics which was paid and organised by Steve as part of the handover. We then leased the furniture for the bedrooms and communal areas.

Lease Option Wolverhampton			
Lease payment	500.00		
Deposit	0.00		
Rent being achieved	1,580.00	**Monthly Costs**	
Money In Purchase		Rent to Landlord	500.00
Refurb	3,790.00	Management Fee (12% of rental)	189.60
Legal Fee's	1,042.00	Maintenance and Voids (10% of rental)	158.00
		Gas, Elec, Water	95.00
Total Money in	4,832.00	Wifi	29.99
		Council Tax	85.00
		TV license	13.00
		Insurance	16.00
		Furniture Lease	78.00
Return on Investment			
Monthly Cash flow	413.41	Total costs per month incl rent	1,166.59
Annual cash flow	4,960.92		
RETURN ON INVESTMENT %		**102.67**	

Another win/win investment. Steve wanted to sell his property in a few years anyway. Now he has an agreed sale price plus he still collects rent every month from us until that day.

I've since spoken with Steve and shown him the pictures of the refurb and he is very happy with the deal. Remember these deals must always be win/win.

The property has been occupied pretty much throughout and achieves £1,580 ppm leaving me around £400 per month profit. These deals are great if done correctly but please never take advantage of anyone with this type of agreement and always adhere to the terms you agreed at the outset.

If you offer things like guaranteed rent then ensure that you pay the rent every month on time irrespective of whether you made profit from the deal that month or not.

Show integrity at all times. If you do what you committed to doing then you will be absolutely fine.

Chapter 13

Which Property Strategy?

Every day I have people messaging me asking me for help, with the most common inquiry by far being which would be the best strategy for me?

Choosing your strategy depends on;

- Available finance
- Risk appetite
- Credit worthiness
- Time
- Skill set

Now without knowing your situation it is very difficult for me to advise which strategy would suit you best as each strategy requires a different level of skill, finance and experience.

Each strategy has good and bad points with different risk ratings and all of these strategies, if you undertake them, please be fully aware of the risks and pitfalls.

This is why education is so crucial. Please don't think you can do this without first becoming educated because trust me you will lose money. I hear people say all the time the money I use to learn I could use for a deposit.

This indeed may be true, but in reality, if you become educated and learn the correct approaches to acquire and fund property, you could gain far more property in the same period of time.

For instance, I met a lady at an event some time ago who refused to pay for any education; she point blank refused saying she did not need this and could learn what she needs to know from YouTube.

Fast forward six months and I received a message from this very same lady. She had been to an auction and purchased a property, not the property she went to buy as she was outbid on the original property she was interested in, the deal she bought was another property going through the auctions.

Her lack of knowledge and experience showed here as she started to bid on a property she had done no due diligence on.

She was now a motivated buyer which is the worst type as she decided to just go for it and ended up as the highest bidder at £182,000.

What shocked me is the fact that someone is prepared to bid and buy a property with no due diligence, no valuations, surveys and no viewing, but she did.

She paid her auction fees and the deposit on the day as the rules of the auction house are that you pay the deposit on the day. These are the terms of auction and you must be aware of this if you choose to purchase from auction, also note that these fees are rarely refundable. When you pay that is final.

After paying the deposit of £18,000 and the additional auction fee's she now had 28 days to complete the purchase and pay the outstanding balance. Online modern methods of auctions give you 28 days to complete from winning the auction whereas in person traditional auctions allow 56 days unless otherwise stated.

Now, this lady had made arrangements for the finance for the original property so just assumed that the finance would be suitable for the next property deal. This was problem number one in the waiting.

Unfortunately, she never reviewed the legal pack correctly otherwise she would have seen that the property she committed to buying was a short lease property which deemed it very much a more complicated investment.

The finance company wouldn't extend the finance for this new deal in a timely manner due to the short lease. The cost of the lease renewal was unclear and the whole situation was a mess.

Either way she needs to pay the balance to the auction house in less than 28 days if she wants to secure the sale otherwise she risks losing the deposit.

The reason for the message to me was to ask if I would lend her the money to buy the deal. Unfortunately, I was not able to assist her due to other financial commitments and after doing basic due diligence on the deal I realised that the deal was not actually very good.

This was incredibly sad and will probably set her back years on her property business as she had now lost just under £20,000.

This tale demonstrates how important education is when embarking on a property business.

I've always been told

"You either pay for your education or you pay for your mistakes"

Your choice, but either way you will pay.

I know people that have invested in their own training and education and gone on to completely dominate their chosen strategy and likewise I know many people who refuse education but make many costly mistakes that training would have prevented or certainly limited.

Let me explain some of the different types of property investments, so you can choose a path that's right for you, your budget, your experience and comfort level.

Please note: Property is an investment and requires calculated risk taking. Your money is at risk and you should only risk money that you can afford.

Single Buy to Lets

A single buy to let property is a property that is let to a single family or person. You have one tenant and one assured short hold tenancy agreement (AST). These are seen as one of the safest ways of investing in property.

They are great for first-time investors looking for a steady return on their investment; depending on the location of the property will depend on the cash flow and capital appreciation. However, generally properties in the south will give you better capital appreciation and cash flow - but will be more costly to purchase. You have to decide on your buying strategy and how much of your available cash you are prepared to risk.

Purchase price and cash-flow are not correlated, for instance a property costing £100,000 may rent out for £650 per month but that doesn't mean that a property costing £200,000 will rent out for £1,300 per month. Just because the property price has doubled, does not mean the rental income will.

I personally would rather spread my risks and buy multiple properties instead of one. I would rather have two properties for £100,000 each as opposed to one property at £200,000. This way you get two of everything, capital appreciation and rental income. Do bear in mind though you will also have two properties to manage and maintain. Let's look at the pros and the cons of each approach, as each strategy has good and bad points to consider.

Good Points

- Less risky strategy
- Single AST contract
- Easier to self-manage
- Tenants pay the utility bills, council tax costs
- Steady income not cash-flow and capital appreciation (area dependent)
- Longer term tenants

Bad Points

- Less profit than other strategies
- If your tenant stops paying their rent, the property has no other income.

Here's an example of a single let deal I found online.

The example shown above is a deal that I found online very quickly and I spent just 15 minutes carrying out some basic due diligence. I have not viewed this deal but it's just an example of what you can find when you look and spend time learning what to look for. The deal above is returning approximately 15% return on capital invested. No bank can give you this sort of return.

Single Let ROI			
Purchase Price	71,500.00		
Deposit	17,875.00		
Mortgage Amount	53,625.00		
Achievable Rent	550.00		
Money In Purchase			
Deposit 25%	17,875.00	**Monthly Costs**	
Tax and Legals (4%)	2,860.00	Mortgage Payments (3%)	134.06
Renovation	3,000.00	Management Fee (10%)	55.00
		Maintenance and Voids (10%)	55.00
Total	23,735.00	Utilities	0.00
		Wifi	0.00
		Council Tax	0.00
Return on Investment			
Monthly Cash flow	305.94	Total costs per month	244.06
Annual cash flow	3,671.25		
RETURN ON INVESTMENT %		**15.47**	

Houses of Multiple Occupancy / Multi-Let

Houses of multiple occupancy (HMO), sometimes referred to as multi-lets, are properties that are designed to provide room rentals and each room will be assigned its own Assured Short hold Tenancy (AST) agreement. The reason these are very popular is that a tenant can occupy just a single room and not have to worry about renting a whole property. Convenience sells as they say, and it's true.

The average length of tenancy for a HMO is two terms of an AST agreement, each lasting six months. The tenant in most cases only has one payment to make each month for their accommodation, as most HMO properties include all bills in the rental payment. A HMO is a great solution for someone moving areas for work or studying and looking for short term hassle free accommodation.

All HMO properties that house five or more tenants must be licensed by the local authority. Properties that are proposing to house more than seven tenants must have planning approval granted by the local authority. You should clarify the specific rules and regulations that affect your property with the local authority as the rules vary from area to area.

Article 4 directives are in effect in some areas and this should be a factor that should be considered when purchasing. In article 4 areas, local authorities have powers to prevent investors converting a single dwelling residential home (C3) into an HMO property (C4). Article 4 is enforced in areas where the local authority deems that there is an over saturation of HMO properties. Areas currently with article 4 directives include Leeds, Liverpool, Birmingham, Wolverhampton and Lincoln. There are many more but these are just a few. Check with your local authority if your chosen area is affected.

You will need to convert the property to comply with regulations and here's some of the changes required but not limited to;

- Fire Doors
- Fire Alarms
- Fire Blankets / Extinguishers
- Signage
- Emergency Lighting
- Smoke Detectors
- Fire Boarding
- Sound Proofing

Rules vary from area to area, so the best way is to speak with the local housing team in the council and ask the HMO officer to assist. They are very helpful and they want compliant landlords and so it is in their interest to assist you.

HMO properties require far more management compared to single buy-to-lets but the cash flow can certainly be higher. Like any strategy you need to work out your risk to reward ratio and be comfortable with the risk and work involved if you choose this strategy.

When considering a HMO property, here's a checklist to assist with the due diligence:

- Article 4
- Planning Permission
- Ratio of Supply vs Demand for Rooms
- Future Developments in the Area
- Business and Job Prospects
- Universities and Teaching Hospitals etc.
- Large Employers

Here's a recent 4-bed Multi-let we sourced for a client in Burnley.

Money Invested		Expenses	
Purchase Price	81500	Mortgage payments	152.81
Deposit (25%)	20375	Management (10%)	147.22
Mortgage Balance	61125	Maintenance (10%)	147.22
Tax & Legals (4%)	3260	Council Tax	87.83
Refurbishment costs	5500	Utility bills	200
Finance costs (if app)	2500		
Total Money In	31635	Total Expenses	735.08

Income Gross		Cash Flow	
Room Rates	85	Monthly Income	1472.20
Number of rooms	4	Monthly Expenses	735.08
Total per month	1472.20	Cash Flow monthly	737.12
Total Per Annum	17666.40	Cash Flow Annual	8845.41
Return on Investment	27.96	%	

It is advisable that an investor should have some landlord experience before taking on an HMO property; in fact, many lenders will not lend to a first time HMO landlord. They will insist on landlord experience.

Good Points

- Higher cash flow
- Multiple income streams from the same property
- High demands in the right area
- Less competition than single lets

Bad Points

- Landlord pays the bills
- Tenants tend to stay for shorter terms
- Requires closer management
- Household disputes between tenants
- Higher maintenance costs
- Higher wear and tear
- Requires additional conversion costs to comply with regulations

Serviced Accommodation

Serviced accommodation apartments are much like hotels without the staff. You would offer your property, either a room or the whole property out for people to book on a nightly, weekly or longer period where they can access the property and treat it like their own for as long as they are there.

The host will provide a cleaning service and laundry and linen service just like in a hotel. You can find many of these on AirBnb, Booking.com, Expedia and other sites to see examples.

Serviced accommodation is fast becoming the new way to find accommodation on weekends away, nights out and holidays. I have colleagues and friends that prefer this type of accommodation rather than staying in hotels as they are generally cheaper than the equivalent quality of hotel.

For instance, in Cambridge City centre, you can book a 5-star reviewed SA apartment for £150 per night whereas a hotel would be in excess of £180. You can see why serviced accommodation is becoming the new trend in property investing.

Extensive due diligence is required for this strategy to ensure the property you use is going to make profit; typically, if the property does not break even at 50% occupancy you should not entertain it. You need to know what your daily rate will be and what your expected occupancy rate will be in the chosen area.

You can use sites such as booking.com, airdna.co, and airbnb.com to assist with due diligence. This strategy is great and can generate a lot of cash, however, it is very dependent on reviews and popularity of the chosen area. Don't underestimate the amount of work required to operate a successful service accommodation property.

Good Points

- Higher cash flow
- Short-term guests
- Huge demand

- Room rates can be changed to suit the supply and demand Very easily
- Very little regulation at present (2022)

Bad Points

- Increasing competition
- High maintenance
- Services required such as cleaners, linen hire etc.
- Increased management required
- Very hands on in early days

Buy Refurbish Refinance Rent / Sell

This is a great strategy and by far my favourite. This strategy is known as the best way to recycle your cash and I'd say the best way to grow a portfolio with minimal investment - the reason being that if you do this correctly you can recycle your cash investment time and time again, meaning you can purchase every three to six months.

Typically, you would be looking for properties that require modernisation or development and these are all over the country and are relatively easy to spot once you've had some training. To maximise the profit from these deals you need to be very good at negotiating, planning and leading a team to get maximum for your money.

Let's look at how to spot these deals, the absolutely best way is to leverage your relationship you have with the estate agents. You should be asking them regularly if they have anything suitable or certainly you should be the first investor they call when the deals come through the door.

Things to look for;

- Tired Dilapidated Property, Old Carpets, Gas Fires, no Central Heating, Dated Kitchens and Bathrooms
- Structural Issues - Subsidence, Cracking, Roof Issues
- Damp Issues
- Potential to Extend or Add Rooms

These are just a few pointers, but basically you are looking for the worst possible looking properties that you know you can add value to. The more problems the more profit can be if done correctly. Please understand it is super important that you do careful due diligence on these deals and really understand the issues the property has and the costs involved to rectify.

A common issue often seen with investors is they completely under-estimate the rectification work and over-estimate the end value both of which can lead to them leaving money in the deal.

Here's an example of a deal I'm working on with an investor at the minute. The property is in Liverpool and the property was obtained through auction.

You can see we purchased the deal for £43,000 plus auction fees and the refurb comes in at £22,400. The property was converted to a three double all ensuite multi-let with a rental income of £1,300 per month.

The cash flow per month after refinancing comes in at £450 - £500 per month but what's really great is the investor was able to withdraw his full investment plus an additional £3,690 which will give this investor infinite returns on his investment. They can now reinvest into another deal.

This is why I love this strategy and will buy all the deals I can finance when they come up. It really is a great strategy but does take planning and lots and lots of due diligence to truly understand the costs and end valuations.

This strategy also favours investor financing as the money can be recycled fairly quickly as you no longer have to wait six months to refinance.

The best way to purchase is cash, followed by bridging finance, however, bridging has additional costs for the lending and can become very costly if you run over the term and so it is imperative you carefully establish your number on the buy refurbish refinance strategy.

Here's the numbers for the deal;

Money Invested		Expenses	
Purchase Price	43000	Mortgage LTV (75%)	78750.00
Acquisition Fees	6220	Mortgage payments (3%)	196.88
Tax & Legals (4%)	1720	Council Tax	87.83
Refurbishment costs	22400	Utility bills	300.00
Finance costs (if app)		Management (10%)	129.90
Total Money in	75060	Maintenance/ Voids (10%)	129.90
End Value	105000	Total Expense	844.51
Income Gross		**Cash Flow**	
Room Rates	100	Monthly Income	1299.00
Number of rooms	3	Monthly Expenses	844.51
Total per month	1299	Cash Flow monthly	454.50
Total Per Annum	15588	Cash Flow Annual	**5453.94**
Profit after Refinance	**3690**		

148

Good Points

- Great way to revive run down properties
- Multiple finance option
- Fastest way of recycling your investment
- Fastest way to build a portfolio with the least amount of investment
- Do it right and you could leave no money in the deal
- Great way to learn the skills of development

Bad Points

- Possible under valuation
- Extended refurbish times
- Increased costings for unseen issues
- Higher fees for finance
- If you run over term bridging fees can cripple any projected returns
- Management issues with build teams

Commercial to Residential

As the title suggests, this property strategy requires you to source a suitable commercial property that could be converted into a residential unit. In most circumstances this will require a change of permission for use of the building for commercial usage to residential usage through a planning application and change of use application via the local authority. Throughout the whole of the UK there are plenty of empty commercial units just waiting for a developer to come along and convert these to residential use.

This is not a strategy for beginners and should not be attempted as your first deal. The risks associated with doing a commercial to residential run far higher than lets say a single let refurbishment. The costs can easily spiral out of control and all manner of problems can occur, hence why I suggest you get some other simpler deals under your belt first.

If you are tackling this strategy then the rewards can be far more lucrative but as with anything the bigger, the reward means the bigger the risk. When sourcing these deals it's imperative you know planning specifications and have a good architect. You also need to be confident concerning planning approval, otherwise you can end up wasting a lot of money.

Good Points

- Higher returns
- Massive potential for increasing in valuation
- Reviving run down commercial properties

Bad Points

- Issues with planning application delaying or ending project
- Increased costs
- Higher purchase costs
- Increased chances or development costs spiralling out of control

Land Development

This is a real money maker; find some land and build some properties on it. Sounds simple I know, but this strategy is for the serious players and those who have experience. You source the land that is prime for development and in an area that has demand for further residential accommodation and you obtain permission from the planning office to build on it.

Once you have the permission, you source the build team to build the properties as per your architectural drawings and then you refinance and rent or sell the properties. This is the biggest money-making strategy of them all in my opinion.

If you know what you're doing, you can really maximise this strategy. The local authority has to release a "local plan" which is published on their website which indicates where they are looking to develop residential properties. Your job is to find land where the council wants to build and then the chances of planning approval will be far higher.

Do not attempt this strategy without the correct advice and training.

Good Points

- Huge profit potential
- Building family homes for a growing population
- Helping governments maintain their house building obligations

Bad Points

- Takes considerable planning
- High costs
- Costs could spiral out of control
- Failed or delayed planning resulting in increased costs for interest in borrowings

Chapter 14

Real Life Case Studies?

Property Sourcing

In this book I've shown how I got started in property and discussed how I began with little money. I genuinely believe that anyone can do what I've done with the right training, guidance, mentoring and action and I'm now going to show you some real life case studies of each of the main strategies.

I first started with Property Sourcing as this required the least amount of money to get started with. As I've shown already in the compliance section you do have an amount to invest in compliance which is approximately £1000.

As of writing this book I have packaged and sold over 450 property deals to investors from all over the world, I've already explained in earlier chapters how I sold my first deal so check that out if you missed this.

The great thing about property sourcing is that you or your team are always looking and analysing property deals and you as an investor have the pick of the bunch of these deals. You see I work with many co deal sourcers as I've systemised my sourcing business and this means my team are looking at multiple deals every week.

As I've systemised the business this means I don't have to be the one looking for property deals. I focus on the business aspect and not the working aspect as much as I focus on the growth and sustainability of the business, not the actual working of the business.

I have a great manager in place and a team of co sourcers which means I can focus on what really makes the money, the investors. You see the biggest issue everyone has when property sourcing is finding suitable investors, which means your efforts in finding great deals could be wasted if you don't have people prepared to buy them from you.

I focus on my brand and my position within the industry so that we attract many investors into what we do and then we can sustain the business and interest from the investors.

Organic growth is the best and currently we're attracting anywhere from 20 - 40 new investors a week. Just this week in June 2022 we gained 27 new investors who all have been through a multi level qualification to access our deals.

List Growth Stats	Rename	
ALL: Contacts Edit	9,667	×
NEW: Today Edit	1	×
NEW: 7 Days Edit	27	×
	Add Another Stat	

Now you may say, well you could easily gain more than this and you're right I could easily attract 100's per week but remember, to get on my list you have to go through a multi level authentication process. This is not just the case of giving me your name and email. I want quality not quantity and the biggest problem you'll have is finding quality investors ready to buy.

When you attend Property Sourcing Intensive we cover in detail the process of qualifying your investors so that they are buyers and not time wasters. I don't deal with time wasters and I ensure very quickly that the people I deal with are serious and ready to buy.

And the proof is in the statistics, the average open rate for a sales email is between 5 - 8% which would be deemed a good result in the marketing world, but because of the way we have set our systems up and how we've trained our investors our open rate is considerably higher.

Email		
Two tidy deals ready to go - cheap B... Sent May 25th at 2:56 PM	Sent	38.8% Opens
Lot's of deals ready to be secured! Sent May 24th at 8:55 AM	Sent	38.9% Opens
15% Short Term 1st Charge Return I... Sent May 23rd at 3:09 PM	Sent	38.7% Opens
Check out the deals we have availab... Sent May 22th at 2:01 PM	Sent	68.5% Opens
Flat Conversions for a £100k RETUR... Sent May 17th at 1:06 PM	Sent	40.8% Opens
Reserve the property you want now! Sent May 17th at 9:01 AM	Sent	39.1% Opens
Get in touch today! Sent May 16th at 2:04 PM	Sent	35.7% Opens
Start your weekend off right - Reser... Sent May 13th at 9:16 AM	Sent	37.3% Opens

You can see our average open rate is nearly 40%, for instance on one of those emails, with the subject line "check out these deals we have available", 60.5% of my database opened the email. That's nearly 6,000 investors, who have all prequalified and gone through multi level authentication.

This is why we can sell deals and sell them quickly and this is why we have made hundreds of thousands of pounds selling property deals. The reality is this, I can sell property deals and get paid in a matter of hours and I can do this without revealing addresses and pictures and sell deals with fees worth thousands over a phone call lasting just a few minutes. When you attend Property Sourcing Intensive live you'll see this first hand.

Property sourcing has allowed me to build my business and as a result of systemisation I have a business which generates me a very healthy income on a monthly basis passively and you can do this too. This business has allowed me the opportunity to find the best deals, which I keep for myself, and the ones I may not be able to complete on we then sell the deals and still get paid.

Here's a few screenshots to show the income we've generated from property sourcing just to settle any scepticism.

£57,244.40   **£40,881.00**

These months are not uncommon and show you that when you do this strategy correctly, with integrity, then you can very easily create a six figure business from property sourcing.

I've created various training events based around property sourcing and I've literally trained some of the best property sourcers in the UK.

Here's one student, Ashley who started working with me in January 2022, and in just 6 months after joining my academy had banked £111,230 from property sourcing through his company.

This business is essential for everyone looking to get into property as it means that you're always out looking for deals, you're always building relationships and meeting new agents. The best deals will come to you from the relationships you build and for me property sourcing was the foundation of my property business.

In the next chapter I'll prove again why property sourcing is such a great strategy and how I came about finding and securing a fantastic buy refurbish refinance deal.

The property was a semi detached property in Bedford just outside the centre. The area was a good area, good schools and has potential for great growth. Bedford was an area that I knew well as I lived in the area for many years.

Real Life Case Studies - Buy Refurbish Refinance

We were currently mid covid, as the property markets were exempt from restrictions, in the sense that we could still carry out viewings. I was making the most of this rule to get out and about and carry out lots of viewings. I was focussing on slightly higher value properties as I had a few investors asking for these types of deals.

I found myself looking for deals around the midlands and south and came across a property in Bedford. Now this property had been on the market for over 60 days and going by the pictures was in a bad state of repairs needing extensive work to make it habitable.

Here's the current floor plan when I purchased it.

And here's a few more images of what I saw when I viewed the property.

Basically the previous tenants had started to carry out interior changes to the structure in order to make it into multiple rooms. The problem was that they had done this without permission from the local authority or their landlord. The tenants had also not been paying rent and were causing a lot of problems with the neighbours and letting the property get into disrepair.

When I viewed the property I was handed a quote from a local company to rectify the damage and issues caused by the previous tenants, now be aware this quote was to rectify the bad workmanship from the previous tenants.

> With reference to your recent enquiry at the above property, we have pleasure in quoting our best price to carry out the following works:
>
> - To supply and install temporary propping.
> - To break out floor area to carry out underpinning as per drawing.
> - To carry out underpinning as per drawing.
> - To reinstate floor slab including insulation and screed.
> - To demolish existing brick / block / timber pillars and remove current steelwork / lintels between existing house and extension and to rear extension wall.
> - To rebuild brick pillars where removed above.
> - To supply and install new steelwork / lintels and padstones to the above new brick pillars.
> - To remove temporary propping.
> - We assume works will be carried out in one continuous phase.
> - For the lump sum of £29,805.00 excluding VAT
>
> Please note no allowance has been made for any remedial works to joists.
>
> Please note we have not allowed for any finishes such as plastering or skirting boards.

The property was owned by Bedford Pilgrim Housing Association and had a local contractors BSG Property services quote to rectify the damage caused which was quoted at £29,805 plus vat, bear in mind this was only to make good and not cover any refurbishment or conversion works.

The asking price was £220,000 and I offered £180,000 which was rejected fairly quickly. I ended up purchasing it for £210,000. My experience told me that the quote above was very much over egged due to the nature of the quote, basically when a local housing association tender jobs, they tend to have preferred suppliers who can often over quote on jobs. I knew I would get this required work carried out considerably cheaper, but to be sure I contacted a former student of mine, who by profession was a structural surveyor.

My thoughts were confirmed and I started the process of buying the house. I planned on using bridging finance to assist with the purchase and I also used my investors database to raise some private finance to assist with the deposits.

So the purchase price was £210,000 and I managed to gain access to the property whilst awaiting completion, to get an accurate build cost from my build team which was quoted at £60,000 including contingency.

My due diligence told me that the end value would be a minimum of £320,000 due to what has been sold nearby,

£ per sq ft price and also discussions with local agents.

5 Caister Road, Bedford MK41 0DF		
Purchase Price		£210,000.00
Legal Costs	Sam Hawkings	£2275.00
Broker Fee	AB Finance Ltd	£449.00
Surveyor Fee	Catalyst Finace	£1870.00
Bridging Facility Fee	Catalyst Finance	£3211.74
Bridging Admin Fee	Catalyst Finance	£550.00
Bridging Chaps Fee	Catalyst Finance	£42.00
Bridging Insurance	Catalyst Finance	£559.00
Bridging Legal Fees	Catalyst Finance	£1800.00
Bridging Solicitor	Anthony and Jarvie	1291
Stamp Duty	Anthony and Jarvie	8000
Bridge Exit Fee		£350.00
	Total	20397.74

So here's a breakdown of the costs that we know so far after obtaining quotes from solicitors and my finance broker.

These are the exact costs which we paid for the set up of bridging and solicitors fees excluding interest for bridging loan; One thing to note, and this is where knowledge and experience comes into these type of deals, the property was uninhabitable and that means you can make a claim to be stand duty exempt. In this case I had to pay the £8000 stamp duty, however, I was able to reclaim this down the line. I did receive a 100% refund of this after I submitted my claim and provided evidence that the property was uninhabitable.

Our interest rate for the bridging finance was 0.89% per month and we had a private lender for £45,000 at 1% per month. We're always happier to use private lending as this often saves us considerable amounts on fees compared to bridging lending.

Here's the breakdown for bridging we obtained, it's worth noting this was taken out right at the start of Covid-19 hence lenders became very cautious about lending so rates may have been increased slightly.

PROPERTY FINANCE

Our Reference: CPF / ACL 15042020

Applicant:		ALC Investment Properties ltd
Security Address:	SP1	5 Caister road, Bedford, MK41 0AD
Charge type:	SP1	1st
Other Security:		PGs from all shareholders with a shareholding exceeding 25% and a debenture
Total Security Value:		£180,000.00
	SP1	£180,000.00
Minimum GDV:		£350,000.00
Purpose of Loan:		Purchase
Max Committed Gross Loan:		£160,587.10
Max Gross Day One Loan:		£117,000.00
Term of loan (months):	12	minimum term is 3 months
Reduced rate of Interest per month:	0.89%	
Standard rate of Interest per month:	2.00%	applies outside of contractual term or in Default
Total Interest due:	£12,495.60	
Total Interest to be Retained:	£12,495.60	To be retained at £1,041.30 per month
Fees to be incurred		
Facility fee:	£3,211.74	Deducted from the advance (2.00% of Gross loan)
Administration fee:	£550.00	Deducted from the advance
Lenders insurance and processing fee:	£559.00	Deducted from the advance (£559 per security)
CHAPS fee:	£35.00	Deducted from the advance
Total Fees to be deducted:	£4,355.74	
Estimated Net loan on Day one:	£100,148.66	(Gross loan – Interest Facility – Fees)
Estimated Net loan on Day one: Serviced	£112,644.26	(Gross loan – Fees)
Estimated Legal fee:	TBC	Plus VAT + Disbursements – **Paid direct to the Solicitors** Further fees may be payable
Estimated Valuation fee:	TBC	Inc VAT – **Paid direct to Catalyst**
Further Development funds (Gross):	£43,587.10	Subject to interim inspection(s) (assuming 3/4 term)
Further Development funds (Net):	£40,000.00	

So our day 1 net was £100,148.66, that's how much we would receive towards the purchase of the deal. Always ask what the day 1 net is and don't go by the day 1 gross as often the fees are taken on the initial lending on the monies.

I still needed to fund the balance as per completion statement from my solicitors which was £212,025.00

This was made up of a personal loan from a private investor of £45,000 at 1% per month and the balance of £66,876.34 was loaned from one of my businesses.

If I needed it I had a further loan from the bridging company for development works of £40,000 if required, however, I chose not to use this to save on interest.

Ok, I now have the keys and the work can get started on the work for conversion. The plan is to make into a 5 bedroom HMO as article 4 is being enforced in Bedford at the end of 2020 and this will mean an increase in rental demand and value.

We informed the local authority of our plan and building control visited the property to assist us with the process of application, fortunately because of the delays with covid building control were being very accommodating and helpful with our plans.

We had to make some structural changes to the property as well as rectifying the structural issues from the previous tenants so we set about doing this in order to make the building safe and get it signed off by building control. This was a fairly straight forward job meaning we had to install some structural steels and get them to approve this.

So I could maximise the floor space we need to open the whole property up and that again meant more structural drawings and steels being inserted. Again building control would have to visit to sign this off. All of this takes time , especially during Covid, as councils are limited with staff at the best of times.

This is the main steel which allowed us to remove load bearing internal walls which in turn allowed us to gain a better use of the floor space.

Now do you remember that quote I was handed earlier when I viewed the property for £29k plus vat, this was to rectify the damage made by previous tenants, well this cost me nowhere near that to sort out, in fact the total cost for the repairs to make good, safe and secure and passed building control for the structural issues were just under £5000.

When you think about this, 43 other people viewed this property and all got scared by this quote. I took one look at it and knew it was an inflated quote from my experience and bought the deal.

Over the next year the property underwent a top to bottom refurbishment, we had many problems, delays and supply issues due to covid but nonetheless fast forward 12 months, the property was now nearing completion and ready to get the final touches.

In total I spent £68,000 on the refurbishment works, we were over budget on this due to a number of factors, the increased costs of materials and one of the builders went into liquidation mid build and was not able to finish the job they started.

This is obviously very painful but in business these things happen.

Total Purchase Price	£212025.00
Refurbishment	£68,000

The total amount of money invested so far was £280,025.

Now, going by my expected valuation of £320,000 this was not the best of deals but certainly not a bad deal. All I needed was a higher valuation and as a high end 5 bedroom licensed HMO I felt we would achieve a higher valuation closer to £380,000.

Here's the finished property.

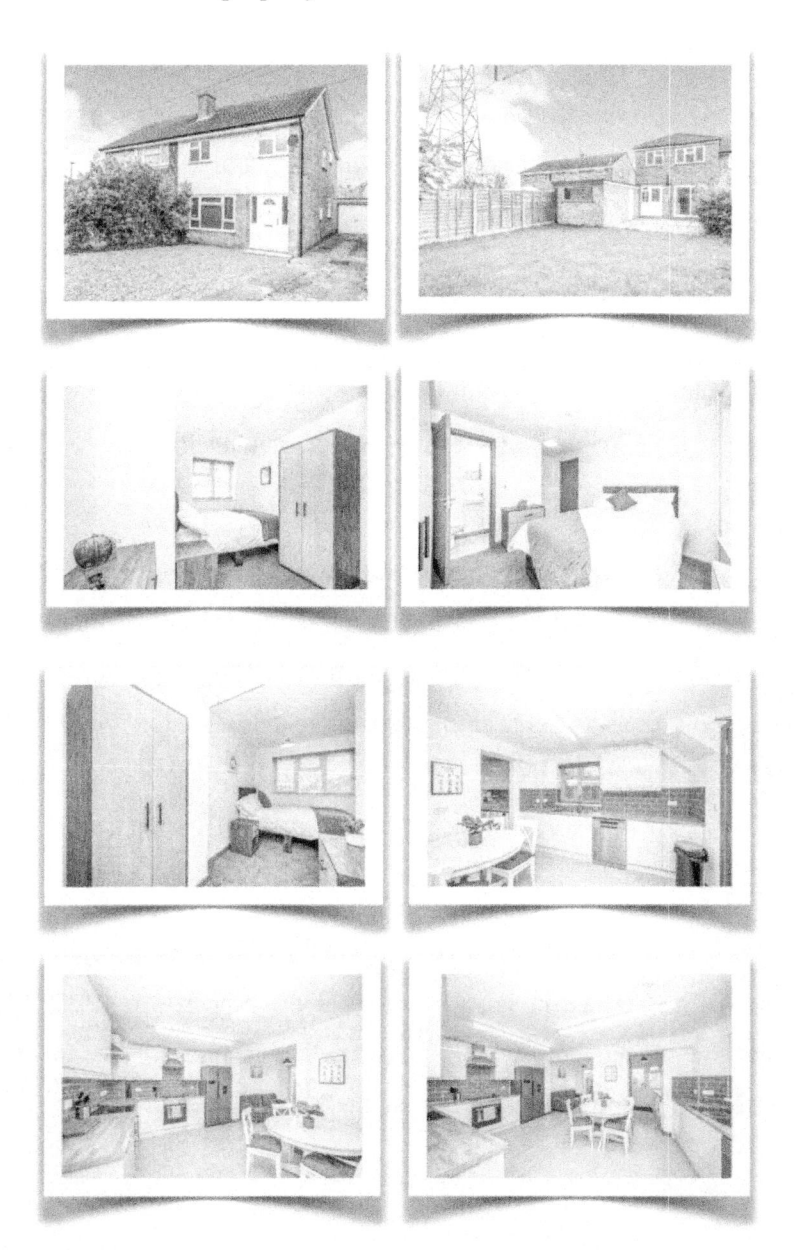

Upon completion we had several local agents come out and view the property in order to see what the market would pay for it and all three agents suggested a selling price of £400,000.

Now, if someone was prepared to pay me that for this property I would snap their hands off. So we marketed the property on the right move and rightly so we have a lot of interest very quickly. I was very strict with who I would allow to view as I didn't want any time wasters, so I insisted on seeing proof of funding if I was to allow them to view.

We had offers from every party who viewed the property and in fact received offers for £412,500 for the property. This was a pleasant surprise and actually we turned this down. The reason for this is because in the short time from finishing to getting online for sale we had been marketing the property on a spare room to let the rooms out.

All five rooms were occupied within a two week window, and we were now in contract with five tenants all paying £650 per room per month. So the passive gross income for the property was £3250. I was now airing more to the side of retaining the property for my portfolio and opting to refinance, so that's what we did.

We had our broker organise the re finance and valuation and the lender agreed to loan on a 75% LTV buy to let mortgage meaning that we left just a small amount of money in the deal.

Now, the property was valued at £400,000 by the lender however, we asked them to lend on a basis of £350,000 as I don't like to be highly leveraged and I was in a cash rich position so I would rather have the equity in the property.

Upon refinance we received just over £260,000 after fees which meant we could pay the bridge lender and joint venture partner back their loans and the balance was paid back to my company.

The property was now rented out and bringing in around £2000 a month profit after all costs and providing a nice healthy return on investment. The property has been completed nearly a year now and the tenants have been there ever since and I've never had any rent or property issues.

This is a great example of a buy refurbish refinance deal and there aren't many investors that wouldn't take this deal. Now imagine you found this deal as a property sourcer and couldn't finance the deal yourself, well you could sell this for a very nice fee and still make profit.

Real life case study - Rent to Rent Hands Free

I met Courtney a few years ago when I was speaking at an event and she had flown from South Africa to learn about the UK property markets. After spending a few days teaching her Courtney realised that the potential and opportunities for the property markets were massive and she needed to be part of it.

Courtney was in a situation where she was at a crossroads in her life, where she had to choose university studying Law or take the plunge and just go for the opportunity and see where things ended up, so with the support of her family Courtney immigrated to the UK and started the steps of beginning her property career.

The chosen strategy for Courtney was rent to rent on a serviced accommodation basis and she was in a fortunate position as her father invested £30,000 to help her get set up in the UK, her plan was to gain multiple serviced apartments within the year.

Being in a position with money to invest and wanting to maximise the cash flow from deals as quickly as possible Courtney opted to use a property sourcer to secure the deals. Through networking and events Courtney built great relationships with other investors and made a great connection with a reliable sourcer who she instructed to find her first deals.

Within a matter of weeks the sourcer had presented several potential rent to rent deals and Courtney was given time to carry out her own due diligence on the deals. After careful consideration and viewing the properties Courtney made the decision to take on her first unit, this unit was in Battersea.

The sourcer charged a finders fee of £3000 for securing the deal, furnishing and dressing the property to a high end came in at £5000, and a £500 for incidentals such as photography which gave a total investment £8500.

The estimated nightly rate for this deal after Courtney carried out her due diligence was £140 which would have given gross monthly income of £3150 at 75% occupancy based on 30 days per month. Properties in this area are considerably higher than 75% occupancy but even at this occupancy rate the property would make approximately £649 monthly cash flow and £7788 annual income.

These figures are all looking great and if all goes to plan then this would be a great return on investment of around 90%.

The great thing about Courtney is the desire for systemisation and all of her properties are fully systemised meaning Courtney is in a situation where she can literally work just a few hours a month managing her managers and checking that everything is working well.

This was a key part of the deal, the deals had to be fully managed so Courtney could focus on bigger opportunities and deals, all whilst enjoying being financially independent with a portfolio of managed serviced accommodation properties.

As of today, Courtney has five up and running and fully managed serviced apartments in London, Windsor and Warwick. In fact Courtney has never actually been to most of her portfolio, the only deal she has ever visited is her London deal and this is the true test of a hands free investor.

Emotions should never come into the deal and this is a real life case study of a young entrepreneurial woman who realised that it's all about the numbers and the numbers are what's important.

Today, Courtney has some seriously impressive opportunities on the table in the UK and abroad and it's all because she has the time to build relationships, network and say yes to every opportunity that comes her way.

Courtney came to the UK to work hard and build a business and she has achieved this very well, especially considering she is just 21 years old. She's a very driven young entrepreneur and a valued member of my business academy.

Today, Courtney has a passive income of just over £3000 per month completely passively meaning she can live her life on her terms and as a 21 year old this is a fantastic position to be in.

By controlling property Courtney has been able to acquire more properties with the investment of £30,000 she raised and this meant higher monthly cash flow, albeit she doesn't own the assets, however, as Warren Buffet states "own nothing and control everything.

Real life case study as a rent to rent Sourcer offering hands free.

Ellen is a truly special entrepreneur. Ellen took some time out of her daily life to travel and learn and this took her all over the world, living in Australia for a year and then settling in UAE working as a teacher in primary education. This was a great opportunity for Ellen allowing her to travel and help children which was very close to her heart.

Her travels took her from her home town of Liverpool to working in the UAE for several years. Whilst at the start this was a great experience it quickly changed. Travelling and working abroad all sounds great but when you're alone in a foreign country things soon started to become very lonely and secluded for Ellen.

Soon, thoughts of returning to the UK were very much in the pipeline and she started to take the relevant steps to make this happen. Making the decision to return to the UK meant that Ellen would need to take a drastic pay cut and we all know that the teaching profession, whilst it can be very fulfilling, is definitely not as easy as everyone thinks. Teaching was fast losing the appeal to Ellen and this led to thoughts of what next?

Property was a great appeal to Ellen and after searching online for inspiration Ellen found herself taking an online training course on property and this is where I met her. She had undertaken an online course and I met Ellen at a seminar I was speaking at. She was a very driven young woman and was in the process of setting up her own serviced accommodation business.

After just a few months, she had managed to secure several properties in Edinburgh, Cumbria and York and these properties were great deals making Ellen a very healthy income on a monthly basis.

At the start, Ellen opted for a managed service for her property in Edinburgh. However after not too long the management company started to let things slip, leading to Ellen taking it back from the company and managing the property herself. The property actually slipped into losing money every month as the management company were just not doing their job well

This was no easy task considering Ellen was a good two hours drive away from the property, but nevertheless she was driven and determined to make this deal work so she set about taking care of this deal and that meant finding a local team for cleaning and changeovers and to deal with any maintenance issues that occurred. In just a few months Ellen took a property that was barely breaking even to making between £750 per month in quiet periods, which was the general monthly profit, to making profit of around £2000 in busy periods.

Another income stream that was proving quite successful for Ellen was property sourcing. I had previously taught Ellen this strategy and this was proving quite lucrative for her. The reason for her success was her approach to sourcing, Ellen provides a complete hands off investment for her investors and this comes from her many real life experiences of actually setting up serviced accommodations for herself.

Let's take one of her investors.

The Investor is from London and wants to invest in serviced accommodation units and took Ellen up on an opportunity for one of her units she had available. The unit was in Cumbria, and this was to be a complete hands free unit..

Ellen offers a full hands free service where she will take care off

- Finding and Securing the Deal
- Negotiating with the owner
- Organising the handover
- Refurbishment
- Furnitures
- Dressing
- Listing the Property
- Organising power teams

You see this is a complete hands off investment for the investor and as a London investor who didn't want to be involved in the process this is ideal.

The costs to the investor for these deals was £8000 per deal. They were so happy with Ellen's services that he committed to taking five units meaning that in that one month Ellen sold deals for a total of £48,000 in fee's for her services. Now of course this is not profit, this is income, after all expenses and costs for furniture there is still a very healthy profit.

Ellen's company provides many investors with these types of deals and I highly suggest you find her on social media to get your next deal. In a later chapter I will introduce you to the 1157 Property Plan and the reason why the book is named as such.

In honour of Ellen's success.. "The 1157 Property Plan"

Chapter 15

Getting Your Hands On The Keys

Control vs Purchase

It's all good learning about the various strategies but how are you going to start acquiring these types of deals so you can benefit from the cash-flow and capital appreciation ? It's important you understand the difference between owning and controlling property and I'm going to discuss both methods in this chapter.

Let's start with taking control of property so you can benefit from the cash flow.

Controlling property is wonderful if used correctly, but is not always the best method of acquiring.

Rent to Rent

This is a great strategy that allows you to benefit from the cash flow of the property without owning the asset. Warren Buffett says

"Own nothing but control everything"

This strategy is a perfect example of this. Think about how many cars does Uber own? How many restaurants do Just Eats own? Exactly! None, but they control and make huge profit by doing so, but without the costs of owning the assets.

A rent to rent deal is where you agree with a landlord that you will take over the management of the property and then you have legal permission to let out the property. You are in effect acting as the property manager where you take responsibility for the running of the property.

Please do not confuse this with subletting as that is breach of contract and therefore deemed illegal; this is not sub-letting. This is property management and you must ensure you have the correct management agreement in place before you commence.

The rent to rent strategy works well if you have a tired HMO landlord who doesn't want to sell, or cannot sell their property - since the property will already have been converted and set up as a HMO.

You can approach the landlord and offer them a fixed rent for a period of time. You take the property and pay a reduced amount to the owner you then let the rooms out and keep the profit.

It's a great low money down strategy and you can get it set up for just a few thousand pounds. It's really important you understand that this is a business and you are entering a contract which means you are liable for the content of that contract whether you have tenants or not.

It's no different to renting a shop, if you don't sell any stock that month you still have to pay your rent.

Some people may question that if the current landlord can't make the property make money, what makes you think you can.

Believe me; there are thousands of landlords all over the country that have just had enough, they are tired of managing tenants, tired of maintenance, costs and constant rule changes.

They may be looking to keep the asset to benefit from future capital appreciation but may be looking for an easier process for collecting rent on the asset, so offering this type of arrangement may work very well for them.

Here's the numbers for a property a colleague of mine took on as a rent to rent agreement. The profit is just over £500 per month from an initial investment of £4,000. The owner purchased the property in 2006 just before the property crash; the property is in negative equity and still not recovered.

This type of agreement works well for this owner.

Rent to Rent

Rent to Landlord	700.00		
Deposit	1,500.00		
Achievable Rent	2,150.00	**Monthly Costs**	
Money In Purchase		Rent to Landlord	700.00
License Fee	600.00	Management Fee (12% of rental)	258.00
Furnishing	0.00	Maintenance and Voids (10% of rental)	215.00
Renovation	3,500.00	Gas, Elec, Water	160.00
Finders Fee	0.00	Wifi	40.00
Deposit	1,500.00	Council Tax	95.00
		TV license	15.00
Total	5,600.00	Insurance	27.00
		Furniture	108.00
Return on Investment			
Monthly Cash flow	532.00	**Total costs per month incl rent**	1,618.00
Annual cash flow	6,384.00	Total costs excl rent	810.00
RETURN ON INVESTMENT %		**114.00**	

Rent to rent is a great way to profit from property without owning it. If you have limited funds, this may be for you. Please ensure you are in a financial position to operate this business correctly which requires certain compliance obligations.

Do this correctly and legally and you could easily be making several thousand pounds per month for a fraction of the outlay compared to standard purchasing methods.

Good Points

- Lower cash outlay
- Try before you buy in the area
- Lower barrier to entry
- No mortgage required
- No requirement for large deposits

Bad Points

- No option to buy the asset
- No capital appreciation
- Harder to secure than a conventional purchase
- Cash flow can be tight if not managed

Lease Option Agreement (LOA)

This property's sale history

Year Sold	Sold Price	Price Difference
2007	£97,000	+237%
1998	£28,700	+19%
1995	£24,000	

This is a great tool that allows you to take control of the property now, with the option to complete the transaction at a later defined date. This is a great way for you, the investor, to assist and help vendors who are in a difficult situation with their property.

This method of acquisition is best used for those vendors who cannot access or do not have any equity in their property and are looking to sell.

There are many vendors across the country who have been attempting to sell their property for many years but cannot, since the properties are in negative equity, even if they sell the property for the asking price they are likely still unable to pay the mortgage off and will actually be left in a far worse situation.

You can find these properties and come up with an agreement with the vendor whereby you take control and responsibility of the property and pay them an agreed monthly amount (lease payment) and then complete the purchase in a defined period of time once the housing market in the area has had time to recover.

Here's an example of a potential lead that I found online in just a few moments.

2 bedroom semi-detached house for sale £89,950
Rawdon Road, Sunderland

You can see the property is for sale for £89,950 but the last registered sale through the land registry was for £97,000 - and this was made in 2007. The vendors have also been trying to sell the property since November 2011. Think about it, what happened in 2008?

The biggest property crash in history. Leading up to this crash there were banks in particular Northern Rock that were issuing loans and mortgages of up to 120% of the property value.

Sold price	Date	Change	Annual change
£97,000	30 Nov 07	238%	14.5%
£28,700	04 Dec 98	20%	5.5%
£24,000	24 Jul 95	-	-

Valuation: £87,000
Value range: £84.000 to £90.000

Let's look at the current market value of the above property using mouseprice.com. The current value is around £87,000 and my prediction is that even if they accepted this as an offer, the vendors would not make any money and would actually probably be left in debt.

This property is prime for a lease option agreement. Your job now is to find out if the vendors would find a solution that could help them.

Lease options must always be a win-win situation, if a lease option will not help the vendor then it is immoral to offer it in my opinion. It is imperative that when you are speaking with any vendor that you do not pressure them into anything and they must have legal representation throughout.

Do not use template contracts to draft this agreement as they will never hold up if they are ever contested. You should treat a lease option the same as if you were buying the property today. Always use a reputable solicitor and ensure you have carried out full due diligence.

A lease option is very similar to a delayed completion, However, with a lease option you have the option not the obligation to complete the purchase. If you were to offer a delayed completion then you must complete the purchase.

Exchange with delayed completion means you agree a sale price for your home with a buyer. When you exchange contracts, the buyer typically pays you an agreed deposit.

However, unlike a normal house sale, completion of the contract and therefore the payment for the property is delayed for a few years.

Lease options agreements mean that a buyer pays you an upfront amount so they have the right to buy your property in the future. The price is agreed on the value of your property now, not when the sale completes.

Under both agreements, the buyer can take over paying your mortgage and make payments either directly to you or to your mortgage lender. They may also take over buildings insurance costs and agree to pay for any repairs to the property.

The above acquisition methods are initially for you to gain control of the property with options down the line, which can be great if you are starting with little investment capital available to you, although these are not for everyone.

If you have investment capital available to you then you can utilise the many lenders on the market and purchase the property straightaway.

Cash Purchase

By far the easiest, quickest and most profitable way to purchase any property asset. You can complete the purchase a lot quicker compared to using financing options. Your legal fees will be reduced and you can negotiate a better purchase price as you are seen as a favoured purchaser by most vendors.

Buy to Let Mortgage

If you want to maximise your cash, you can opt for a buy to let mortgage where you will typically have to contribute around 25% of the purchase price as a deposit with the lenders making up the balance. Rates vary; however, you can expect to obtain a deal at a rate of 2-3% interest. You will be charged additional costs for arranging the finance such as a broker fee.

To obtain a buy to let mortgage I'd advise you speak with an independent mortgage broker. You will typically have to pay a fee upfront for their services and you will also have to pass lending criteria checks including but not limited to credit report, income status and employment status - however the lending is not solely based on you. The property and the income from the property is also considered.

Bridging Finance

A great option if you are following the buy refurbish refinance strategy where you are buying a heavily discounted property to refurbish to increase the value to then sell or refinance. Bridging finance is essentially a high interest short term lending facility. The fees can be expensive and if you exceed the term of the loan the fees become excessive. You should only use this lending source if you are fully aware of the consequences of not settling the loan on time. I currently have a property refurbished using part bridging; here's the figures:

Purchase price   £210,000

Gross done up Value   £350,000

Bridging Facility Fee	Catalyst Finance	£3211.74
Bridging Interest	Catalyst Finance	£12495.60
Bridging Admin Fee	Catalyst Finance	£550.00
Bridging Chaps Fee	Catalyst Finance	£35.00
Bridging Insurance	Catalyst Finance	£559.00

The interest is charged at a rate of 0.89% per month in term and if we go outside term it rises to 2%. The minimum term is 3 months and maximum 12 months. We plan on paying back within 6 months so the below charges for interest will be halved to approximately £6,200.

Bridging finance is easier to obtain and quicker, but comes at a price. The build of the risk is on the property and not the borrower. Be careful with using bridging finance and please seek professional advice from a qualified mortgage broker before applying for this type of borrowing.

Private Investor Funding

This is a great way to raise finance if you have people in your network who have money sitting in the bank earning them very little interest. You can offer to pay them a higher interest rate and if they trust you and you can agree terms, then this can be a great deal for both parties.

I've utilised this method of borrowing on several occasions to assist with deals.

I borrowed £25,000 from an overseas investor who I've assisted in purchasing property in the UK through my sourcing business. I wanted to raise the capital for a buy refurbish deal I was working on so I put a proposal together for an investor. I did this in the form of an investor pack which details all of the particulars of the deal and what the money is being used for.

The agreement was that I would borrow the money which would be paid to my limited company and my limited company would repay the money 6 months later with interest payable at 1% per month. I borrowed £25,000 and paid back £26,500.

The total cost for me was £1,500 and I used this money to fund the deposit for a property which I refurbished and refinanced. The investor is happy to make the interest whilst I am happy as I completed on a property.

Always use a legal contract if you choose to use this method of borrowing and ensure you and the lender are fully aware of the risks involved.

However you choose to fund the deal, it is important to always be getting a discounted purchase price. You must learn how to negotiate and always be looking for below market value deals.

Below Market Value

I have a friend called Scott, he is an Australian investor with fourteen properties in Brisbane and he works and lives in the UK; all his properties are managed locally and he literally has nothing to do with them. He's very experienced and has seen most things that could go wrong and Scott always said to me,

"Alasdair, you need to understand you make your money when you buy not when you sell, buy the right property for the right price and you are set"

This has always resonated with me and stuck in my head, 'You buy the correct property and negotiate the correct price and then you're set for life'. It may mean that it takes you longer to find the right deals but believe me it will be worth the effort in finding them. Everything is easier when you don't pay over the odds for the deals. If you can find a property deal that you can secure below its true market value, you are instantly in profit. It's the very best way to start off on a good investment. There are many of these properties around and here are some reasons why a vendor may allow a below market value offer purchase price.

- Facing Repossession
- Probate Sale
- Separation
- Needs Refurbishment
- Moving Abroad
- No outstanding Mortgage

Combining a below market value purchase with any other strategy is like the icing on a cake and as an investor, you should be actively looking to get the best possible purchase price on any deal you're looking at.

A great place to look for these deals, particularly those that are direct to vendor is on Gumtree; generally only people desperate to sell list their properties on Gumtree so it's a great place to start and find direct to vendor leads. You will more likely be able to get a below market value offer accepted when dealing directly with the vendor.

If you want to get good at negotiating then the first thing you need to do is start getting good at listening. Listen to the vendor when doing your viewings, particularly if they are distressed sellers and needing to sell quickly - as they will generally tell you everything you need to know before you ask, if you just listen.

I always find out why they are selling and try to find the best option by which I can help them in the best way possible. I am not there to steal their property from them, I'm there to offer a solution to their problem. When you help people get what they want then you will generally get what you want but I think it's really important to come from a position of service and not as a motivated buyer.

Here's an example of a deal I found via Gumtree recently; the property was being advertised with just one picture and on the market with offers in the region of £85,000. The property required around £8,000 - £10,000 spending on it and had been vacant for around 12 months as the owner had passed away and the property was now being sold by the family.

During the viewing, I was listening to the vendor, listening to the problems that they had dealing with the property and trying to sell it. There had been several sales which fell through and they just wanted it sold and sold quickly. He had listed the property at 'Offers In the

Region of' (OIRO) £85,000 - so I asked him this question and then said nothing.

> *"If I can guarantee you a sale with no delays, what's the lowest price you will sell it for?"*

After a moment, he said if I could act quickly, no messing about and complete asap then he would take £67,500, the reason they reduced it was they wanted a quick sale and they knew it needed work to bring it up to standard.

The thing is, I would have paid more but because I kept quiet and let them tell me their lowest price first, I got the property at a below market value by at least £15,000.

I didn't take advantage of him or hard sell him, I simply viewed the property, listened to their problems and then asked a very simple question and let them answer.

I was happy with the purchase price and so was the seller. I accepted his lower offer and shook his hand on the agreed price of £67,500.

I offered this deal to my investor's database and found him a cash buyer within 24 hrs. The property completed 6 weeks later and is now in the process of being refurbished. You see when you help people and offer value, you get a better outcome. Remember whenever you view property always come from a position of serving and not a position of a motivated buyer.

Chapter 16

Getting Started on Your Journey

After assessing all the strategies and your financial situation, I would make a decision about what strategy you would like to pursue and then I would look for an area where that strategy will work.

Let me briefly assist you with finding an area.

Area

Choose an area you would like to invest in; this may be somewhere close to you or the other end of the country. It really doesn't matter where the property is unless you plan on self-managing the property.

I would look for areas that have a good infrastructure, universities, good job prospects, good median income and high employment rates.

You can use google to find all this information out. Once I have preselected an area that I would like to invest in, I then visit the area and take a look around, stay over for a day or so and see what the area is like both day and night.

I always go and meet some estate and letting agents to ask their opinion on the area.

They are generally local experts so take notes. Here are some pointer questions to be asking:

- Can you tell me the areas that are working well and the areas that are simply no-go areas?
- What is the average rental income for (x) street?
- What type of tenants are we likely to get?

- Average rental income?
- How many properties do you currently manage?
- What is your delinquency rate of tenants in arrears?

You want to build a relationship with the agents in the area, so that they want to work with you. They are your best source of a power team in the area and if you look after them, they in turn will look after your property and tenants.

Remember not all areas work well for all strategies, for instance HMOs work very well in certain parts of the country but will simply sit empty in others.

So, you must ensure you do extensive due diligence on your chosen area for your chosen strategy. Always check for supply and demand.

This is just a brief overview on choosing an area; once you decide on a strategy then you should focus heavily on doing extensive due diligence for the area before committing financially to any deals there.

Properties

You will find properties for sale listed on many places online. Mostly, you'll use Rightmove or Zoopla for your property sourcing. It's important that you become good at assessing property before you even leave your house. Otherwise, you'll end up looking at hundreds and get nowhere. Learn what to look for when you are finding the leads online by doing basic due diligence before you book a viewing such as;

- General Condition
- Idea of Refurbishment Required

- Condition of Exterior / Roof (use Google street view)
- Location / Amenities / Rentals Demand / Supply
- Type of Tenants
- Average Rate for the Area
- Flood Risk / Known Local Ground Issues
- Planning Restrictions
- Rules and Regulations
- Valuation and Current Comparable Properties Nearby

When you get good at looking you will be able to do these checks very quickly and you will also have a good understanding of the properties in your chosen area. You should build a good rapport with local estate and letting agents so when you have a potentially good deal you can call them up and ask their opinion on it.

Only once I have verified the above, will I attend a viewing. When you view, I'd recommend taking someone who knows what they are looking at if you don't, so you can assess the property condition correctly and cost any refurbishment works.

Here's a list of the basic checks;

- Exterior condition - check for leaning, cracks, roof line, guttering, windows, doors, brick work inconsistencies.
- Interior condition - check for damp, peeling, bulging walls, leakage, odours, subsidence, uneven floors.
- Bathroom - age and condition, water pressure, wall tiling, leakages, drainage

- Kitchen - Age and condition, water pressure, boiler condition and paperwork / service sticker, pipe work condition, drainage, work surfaces, damp under sink.

- Electrical System - Check for any service updates, usually on a sticker in the fuse box, new or old fuse box, condition of wiring - is it tidy or messy? General condition of wall sockets and light switches.

- Overall Property Condition - decoration, carpets, floors, windows, skirting boards, doors and door linings and stairs.

It is essential that you take someone who knows what they are looking at if you are not confident in assessing a property. If you have a refurbishment that needs quoting for then you need to get this quote as accurate as possible at this stage, so you know how to stack the deal up and ensure that the deal is a financially viable option for you. Remember at all times due diligence is your friend and this should become second nature to you as a property entrepreneur or investor.

The quickest way you can accelerate your property journey is to get around like minded people who want something similar to you, your environment is crucial so ensure you're around the best people for your business.

Next, get educated. You'll accelerate your journey considerably when you have the right education and I believe we offer the best value and most comprehensive property education in the UK. Quite simply there is no other trainer providing the amount of value we are for the investment required.

Check out what we can help you with by visiting the website

www.alasdair-cunningham.com

Chapter 17

Forget the BS and Just get on with it!

On a poll I posted on Facebook when I was researching this book, I asked what are peoples' biggest reasons stopping them from following their dream of becoming a property investor or entrepreneur.

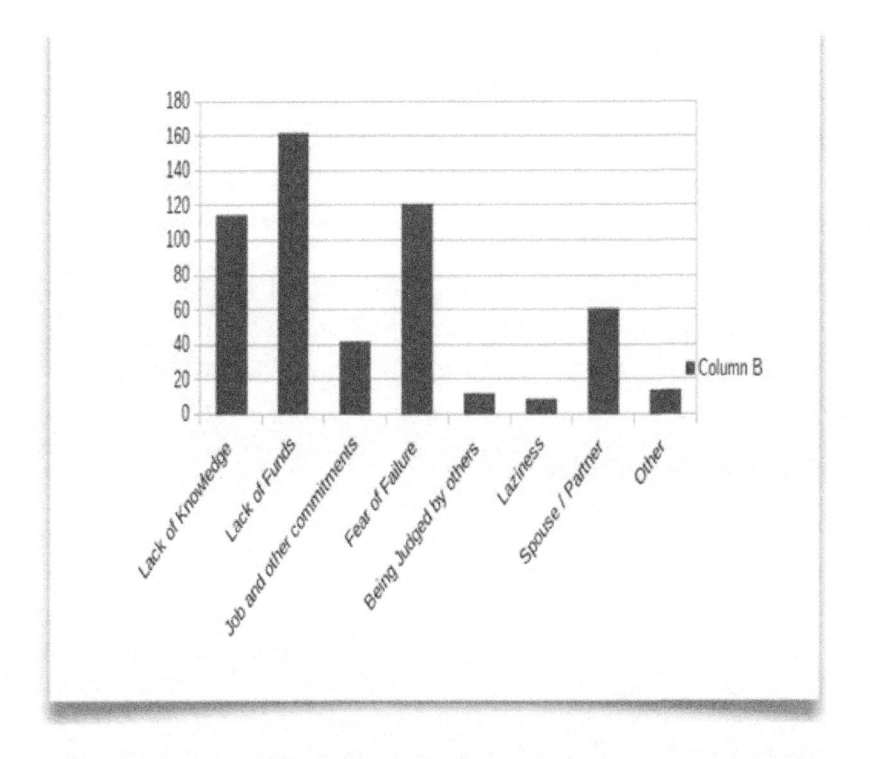

Let me show you the results: 536 people took part, all of whom were targeted due to their interest in property investing or becoming a property investor. The biggest issue was lack of funds, followed by fear of failure and lack of knowledge.

I've explained how I became an investor without having lots of money and there are loads of ways to gain knowledge. I want to talk about the two biggest things that delayed me.

Fear of Failure

The fear of failing is what has always stopped me really excelling in business and because of this, I never truly put 100% into any of my previous ventures. My previous businesses were ok, I made a good living out of them but they never really exploded.

Why?

My fear of failure stopped me from growing them, it stopped me from pushing for that big contract, it stopped me taking risks that my gut told me to take, but my mind was telling me it won't work.

The thing with failure is you have to fail to win and every entrepreneur has failed at something. Failures bring very valuable lessons which make you grow in knowledge, experience, and your mind.

The more you learn, the more you earn and failing will be one of the biggest learning curves you will go through.

Donald Trump, love him or hate him, has failed several times, but he was President of the US - and a very successful businessman. Duncan Bannatyne, Lord Sugar and many others have all at some point had a business fail.

They have all risen from failures to be great successes. Look at Ray Kroc from McDonald's; he had numerous failed start-ups prior to building the McDonald's brand worldwide.

My point is, get over it just like these people did, stop worrying about failing, learn as much as you can about your chosen path and just do it.

Believe me, on my journey, I've had my up and down days when I cannot believe that my life is changing so much, days where I feel the bubble is about to burst and it's all been a dream.

My life has become so busy over the last few years and it's non-stop which I absolutely love. I thrive when I'm busy.

Please don't let irrational thoughts ruin your potential.

When I first got involved in property, I set myself some goals.

- 1 x HMO Purchase
- 1 x Lease Option Property
- Raise £30k from an Investor
- Package and sell 12 deals to Investors
- Build an Investors List of 100
- Grow in Confidence
- Immerse Myself in Property

The twelve months goal shortly became my three-month goal after my mentor said twelve months was too long. I am pleased to say I failed at this. I achieved everything on the list in 3 months apart from raising £30k from an investor.

But I'm pleased that I failed.

"I would rather set my goals high and miss than set them low and hit"

I might not have the £30k from an investor within the 3 months but I hit every other goal! I have grown in many areas such as business, mind, knowledge, ability, confidence, heart and friends.

Today I am a changed person, have a completely different mindset and outlook on everything and so please remember it's good to fail sometimes!

Incidentally I did successfully find an investor prepared to fund any deals I find as a joint venture. As yet I've not needed his help but the fact that I have that is great, but I'm pleased I succeeded in raising £30,000 from an investor a few months later.

Being Judged by Others

You will lose friends on your journey.

Why?

Because most of your friends want you to fail. True. When they see you out shining them, jealousy kicks in. They will try to derail you on your journey. They will judge you for attending a "Property Seminar".

I know people who have attended seminars and told no one they were coming and I asked why? And their reply is that their family or friends just don't get it.

Most people don't get it as they are happy with a mediocre life. You and I are not and that's why we will excel.

Lots of people will happily moan and bitch about their situation, but when it comes to the crunch and they have an opportunity to make their situation better.

They simply are too lazy, risk-adverse or comfortable to do anything about it. Taking the decision to better your life means you are going to have to make sacrifices which most people are not prepared to do.

Being judged by others was a big concern for me and I would say a big reason why I took so long to take the plunge and just do it. I didn't want to be told, "I told you it wouldn't work", or be mocked and laughed at if things went wrong.

My insecurities and anxieties were going nuts at the start of my journey. I am now more determined than ever to prove these people wrong. If you have people around you dragging you down then get rid of them.

If they cannot support you without question, then you don't need them in your life. You need to be around people who think like you and want to help you reach your goals.

You will gain far more by having a few like-minded people in your life than having negative people around you. That's why I love networking; I attend regular networking events as the room is generally filled with people who all want to help one another, are all driven and all looking to meet people with the same drive. I've done a lot of business with contacts I met at networking events.

I was essentially a closet property investor in the beginning. I didn't want to tell people what I was up to and I now look back and wonder why I was like that. I know it was my fear of being judged and mocked, you see I was fighting my own confidence and anxiety battles and worried a lot about what people thought about me.

This is something a lot of people suffer from and I promise you, it will not be as bad as you think it will. Now I have stepped out and told the world what I am doing, I am more confident, proud and content with myself and my achievements.

A couple of comments were made to me about the training I embarked on when I first started. I'm sure we have all heard this;

> *"If he is so successful why is he training others to do the same?"*

Imagine saying to the bosses of Apple,

> *"If you make so much money from selling your phones, why do you sell Macbooks?"*

Only those with a poor broken mindset would ask such stupid questions. These are the same people that complain that the rich get richer while the poor get poorer. I've become very impatient towards people who are critical of those looking to do something different to what society expects of you.

I've had many comments and "digs" about spending money on personal development and property education.

Mostly from people that have racked up many thousands more in student loans to go to university, only to leave university and not even use their qualification. These same people spent tens of thousands to go to university to then work a normal everyday job for the rest of their lives.

I'm not against university at all, however I prefer real life self-education that will make me a fortune instead of formal education that will make me a living. Each to their own I say and I don't judge anyone for their chosen path but in turn I don't expect to be judged for my chosen path.

I have no time for these people and have become very intolerant of them. If people are critical of me then for me it's very simple; I cut them loose. You either support my ambition or leave, it's that simple. You can disagree with me and still support me which I'm fine with.

Chapter 18

What's Your Purpose?

This is something I've always really struggled to understand, I've never really been spiritual and honestly thought that when I heard people banging on about their why I used to just think come on nobody really cares so just get on with it and stop with the sympathy, attention seeking, oh isn't that sweet bullshit. The reality is nobody really cares about your "why".

However, what I will say is nobody needs to care about it other than you, and in all honesty when you truly understand why you're here, then the how will become considerably easier. I truly believe everyone has a bigger and more rooted purpose than just to make money and your job is to actually understand what your purpose is.

It may well be just to make money, but I'll ask you, why do you want to make money?

Of course you'll all answer the obvious answer such as to support my family, pay bills, have nice holidays, spend time with loved ones etc but that's just surface level. You'll need to dig deeper if you're to truly understand your purpose because frankly you can make money in a job, so why not just get a job?

The reality is this, business and property is incredibly hard work and you're going to really understand why you're here if you're to succeed because you'll be tested time and time again and if your purpose is not strong enough it is very easy to quit and just accept what you get.

I do an exercise at my advanced training events called "Seven levels deep" and this is all about truly understanding your purpose and why you're here. You can do this yourself if you want to, however, I highly recommend you experience this exercise in person as it will have more impact.

So I want you to ask yourself seven times why you're here, for instance, in this example, which is a fairly common response, I ask seven questions to get to the real reason why they're starting a new journey.

(Question) Why?

Answer - I want to make money because then I could ensure my family is taken care of and they won't have to worry.

(Question) Why couldn't you just get a job? Why does having a business mean you'll be able to support your family better?

Answer - Because a job is not secure as I've been let go and made redundant several times now and that has caused us serious financial difficulties in the past and I don't want my children to have to worry that they could be let go tomorrow because I want them to feel secure in themselves.

(Question) Ok, so it's important you feel secure with your finances? Why is that?

Answer - Because growing up my family was always struggling with money and I always remember hearing my parents argue about money a lot and I think that's why they separated and for me this was a very tough time in my life.

Now, you get the picture, ask yourself at least seven times why you're doing this? And push yourself to come up with the real reasons. This is a really powerful exercise to do but you need to be honest with yourself.

In the above example you can tell it's not just about making money, they want to make money because of an emotional tie to money or actually the lack of money as it brings back pains and past trauma about their childhood and the issues struggling financially brought to their life.

You'll find that serial entrepreneurs may fail in a particular venture but trust me they're soon at it again as the motivation is not just money but rather what money can provide for them, their family or chosen beneficiary. Your purpose has to be bigger than you, if it's not then it's very unlikely that you'll ever succeed.

People ask me often why I do what I do, and for me I have always wanted more from life than just a job, in all honesty failing in a business doesn't scare me. Getting a job does and I'll do whatever I have to do legally and ethically to make sure I never have to get a normal job. Entrepreneurs have an inner drive that creates this beast from the inside, where normality is not accepted and that's often the reason why many entrepreneurs have had disruptive personal lives.

I've never wanted to settle for normality and I don't want my family to either. For me, everything I do is for my family and that means nothing or nobody will prevent me from achieving what I want to achieve and this doesn't mean I won't fail. Not at all, this just means that I'll be giving everything I've got to my business in order to achieve "choice"

Choice is the word we all work towards.

The choice to travel when you want.

The choice to work when you want.

The choice to sleep in one day without worry.

The choice to wake up when you finish sleeping and not when the alarm tells you to get up.

The choice to help others when they need it.

The choice to choose what I do today.

You see, I want choice in my life and quite frankly if you work in a normal job that choice is considerably restricted and this is why I started my first business which we spoke about earlier in this book.

I've been in business for nearly 20 years now and I wouldn't change a thing about my businesses because I've learnt from every success and every failure and all of these have created the results we have today.

The reality is this, I can choose what, where and when I do anything, and if I choose not to then I don't, and this choice has made it possible for me to start my training business because I have time to do it, because of systemisation in my businesses.

Helping others achieve their version of success has become a big part of my life and I wouldn't change it for anything. I believe I was destined to be on stage helping and serving others and I get great pleasure from it. Today I've helped thousands of people through my events, training and books.

I've been fortunate to have been invited to share my knowledge and experience on the world's stage which was a great honour for me, this is something that I worked towards for several years and now I can say that I've become an international speaker and trainer and the fulfilment that this brings is immense.

Being in a position where I can help others change their life, the same way I did, is probably the most fulfilling experience I've experienced and makes all the sacrifice and hard work worthwhile.

So whatever your purpose is always remember that's why you're doing what you're doing and whenever you feel like quitting remember your purpose. As I said, a big part of why I do what I do is for my two girls, Isobel and Yazmin. I don't want them to struggle financially or ever worry that they cannot enjoy their life because of a lack of choice.

Purpose will keep you going whereas just making money will not and that's been proven time and time again. You'll see many successful people who end up with severe depression and mental health issues when they get off the carousel, they hit their targets and often feel like something is missing.

The old saying of enough is never enough is relevant here because that's what happened to me. I became financially independent and was able to choose my life and although this sounds like a dream, in reality it's a very boring existence, albeit I can afford to keep myself entertained.

But there are only so many holidays, luxuries and experiences you can spend money on, it soon becomes a little blah, and this is why it's so important that you have something bigger to achieve than just making money and that's why I train and help people through my training.

Take my signature personal development training event called "Tell The World", this program is designed in a way to push you to your limits and has helped hundreds of people change their lives. I only run this four day experience twice a year and these four days will excel you into a new you.

My training events are really important to me because of the results that we have achieved in helping others achieve their results, for instance.

Make sure you're following my instagram to keep up to date with more success students, as we post success students every few days from our training. Seeing my students succeed is a massive motivator to me and part of my purpose. My training has helped many people achieve what they want and that's one reason why I do what I do.

One of the reasons that I see why people don't achieve what they want to achieve is generally down to them. That's the truth, if you're reading this and always finding excuses for your lack of success then you need to look closer to home because trust me the only thing stopping you is actually you.

My task when you work with me is to get you to understand just how great you are and just how capable you are and that's why I love training people, and when I train you, take my word that you'll get the absolute best from our team and we will show you just how great you can be so I'd highly suggest coming along to our free event and see what we can achieve together.

Come along and enjoy the process just like my success students did and maybe you'll be my next success.

The link for TrustPilot is at the end of the book in contact us.

My purpose has driven to many great achievements and inspired me to say yes, even when I was screaming no. The reality is this, I would never have achieved what I have done if I was just after money, because trust me the journey has been incredibly difficult, but worth every moment.

- Property portfolio consisting of single lets, BRRR deals and HMOs. Currently due to complete on a further two in the coming week.
- Passive Income allows the choice to do what I want.
- Deal sourcing business averages £36,000 per month which is fully systemised with staff.
- 10,000 strong investors list who buy deals or enter joint ventures with me on a weekly basis.
- World wide public speaker - I train and speak at events several times a month throughout the UK and Asia to hundreds of people each time.
- Award Winning Entrepreneur and Speaker.
- Best Motivational Speaker in the UK 2022.
- Trained thousands of people on how to get started in property and follow in my footsteps.

There is more but hopefully that is enough to inspire you to just take action and step out of your comfort zone a little to see where your journey will take you.

These are just a few reviews you can see from my clients and these are the people who keep me going on my journey. I respect and value every one of them.

You can check out the rest of my reviews on TrustPilot, the link is on my website.

George Ward
GW 2 reviews GB

★★★★★   26 Feb 2022

1st event on the business academy !

1st event on the business academy !
Unreal as all the events Alasdair runs,
Gave me clarity on the direction I'm going!
Can not wait for the next event And my success ! Watch this space

---

Ashley Toft
3 reviews GB

★★★★★   17 Feb 2022

Can't believe this is free

The course creation blueprint is insane value for a free training course. Alasdair provides a step by step basis on how to choose your topic create a funnel and monetise what you do in a systemised manor.

Would easily pay for this!

Thomas Grierson
4 reviews GB

★★★★★   26 Feb 2022

The Business Intensive Blueprint is excellent!!

The Business Intensive Blueprint has been integral for my pivoting perspective to achieving success

---

John Morton
1 review GB

★★★★★   26 Jun 2022

Two Day Business Mastery

Just attended the 2 Day Business Mastery course hosted by Alasdair and it was yet another 5star event!. With no content apart from a skeleton to the 2 days Alasdair focused on our (and our businesses) problems and crafted an organic programme addressing these issues and making sure each and every one of us knew the actions to take to resolve.

Conclusion

I want to leave you with some action steps, so you can start straight away and I sincerely hope everyone reading this follows these:

Step 1

Educate, Educate, Educate.

Give yourself the gift of learning something you don't know. Please start educating yourself today.

The best start would be to visit my online training platform www.alasdair-cunningham.com.

We also host several free events that you can attend live.

They're completely free to attend and you will learn a lot, plus I'll be there and I can answer any questions you have.

www.alasdair-cunningham.com

Step 2

Implement TODAY.

Whether you attend an event, read a book or watch a YouTube video, you must learn to implement and put into action what you already learned. It is no use learning loads and doing nothing.

Watch me on YouTube "Alasdair Cunningham".

Follow me out on Instagram - alasdair_cunningham

Step 3

Ignore the doubters and little voices. Push on even if you are criticised. Push every day. Cut them out of your life, or certainly only see them on your terms.

Step 4

Step out of your comfort zone. Do something every day that makes you feel uncomfortable. This could be something as simple as the next time you are on the train saying hello to the person sitting next to you. Get comfortable being uncomfortable.

Whenever I get offered an opportunity, I say YES. I'll figure it out after.

Step 5

Attend property networking events, they are very cheap to attend and you will meet many people just like you there.

Network like crazy, remember to add value to other people before you ask for something.

Step 6

Get your finances in order so if you find a great deal you are prepared. Once you have assessed your financial position and spoken with a mortgage broker, decide which strategy would best suit your needs and finances.

Once you decide on the strategy, learn as much as you can about it.

Become a master of one strategy and not a jack of all.

Step 7

Have fun, enjoy the journey and accept that you're going to come up against closed doors and struggles but believe that if you can push past these, you will look back with no regrets.

Step 8

Tell everyone what you're doing, you never know who among your circle of contacts may be looking for someone to joint venture with on a deal.

Step 9

When you have any success, then celebrate. Let me know so I can celebrate with you especially if it is as a result of this book.

Thank you very much for getting to the end and I truly hope every single person who has made it here gets the result they deserve. Please take action and get out there.

Step 10

Tell The World what you're doing, they need to know. Now most people shy away from this because they fear other people's opinions but just go for it and do it. You never know who is listening and what opportunities may come your way.

Stay In Touch

I'd love to hear of any success you have and I really hope I have inspired you to take action and step out.

If you have enjoyed this book and found it helpful please let me know and perhaps leave me a review on amazon if that's where you bought it or on trust pilot. You can reach my team on the following channels

Website - www.alasdair-cunningham.com

Instagram - @alasdair_cunningham

Email - team@alasdair-cunningham.co.uk

YouTube - Alasdair Cunningham

I welcome you to attend my free property training event, we run these regularly and you can get your free tickets by securing your free tickets on the website www.alasdair-cunningham.com

Over the course of this free event I will show you just how possible it is for any everyday person to make huge sums of money from the property industry. I did and I'm no different to you and that means you too can achieve the same level of success.

The event is for you if you're looking to kickstart your journey into the property industry which is one of the most lucrative professions available. This event will be the start of your very lucrative property career if you're prepared to commit and take action. I did and it changed everything for me so come along and let me show you how.

You will learn how to;

- Scale to £100,000 a year from Property just like my students do regularly.
- Source and secure high cash flowing property deals for passive income.
- Send an email and get paid thousands in a matter of hours.
- Build your list of ready to buy investors to buy your deals and joint ventures with you.
- How to build a sustainable business that lasts more than just one deal.
- How to find high cash flowing assets to build generational wealth.
- How to raise cash for deposits.
- How to avoid losing thousands by making costly mistakes.
- And so much more

This event will be the start of a very profitable venture for you and there is no other trainer able to offer you what I can offer you. Come along and see for yourself. What have you got to lose - nothing but everything to gain.

Get your Tickets just visit www.alasdair-cunningham.com

Come with high expectations and be prepared to have not just your mind blown with what's possible but the drive to make the possible a reality for you. Many have already and you could be next.

About The Author

Alasdair Cunningham is an everyday family man who decided after 18 years of grafting that there must be an easier way to earn an income. He sought out to find it and succeeded.

His wife Lisa has stood by his side throughout the ups and downs of his current and previous businesses, for this she deserves a medal. Lisa has always supported Alasdair even though at times thinking he was daft. They have two daughters Yazmin, who works in law and Isobel who is doing her studies at upper school and excels in mathematics.

Alasdair regularly gets invited to speaking engagements to share his story from stage and considering that he would struggle to speak in front of a small audience a few years ago shows you just how much he has grown in confidence and strength.

Lisa, my ever-supportive wife, who has stood by me even when she hasn't agreed with what I am doing. You'll forever be in my heart and I couldn't have done this without you.

I have also made countless new supportive lifelong friends, many of whom have been there throughout my journey. We've shared many experiences, nights out and enjoyed the journey together on the way. You know who you are and honestly you've pulled me up when I was at my lowest.

A few of my students and colleagues wanted to add to this book so I gave them an opportunity to share a few words.

Alasdair is a serious action taker, he knows what he wants and does whatever it takes to get there. With that being said he is certainly not a cut throat. He's a really nice, genuine and loyal guy, the sort of person who will always be there for you when you need him. I'm proud to call Alasdair a friend - Russell Leeds

With Alasdair's help, I purchased 4 x HMO properties. Alasdair was very open and honest throughout, and I'm pleased to say 16 out of the 18 rooms are now occupied and achieving a higher than expected income. I have no doubt the other rooms will fill very quickly, Great work Alasdair and I can't wait for the next deal. - Michael Yong

I met Alasdair in September 2017 at a training event, my first thoughts were that he was a very genuine and nice person, a few things I picked up on were that he was quite cynical, sceptical, and full of self-doubt. Alasdair is a smart guy and I have witnessed Alasdair grow both as a person and in business. He has become a lot more self-confident and started to believe in himself. Congratulations on your success and personal growth - Stuart Brown

You'll soon identify that integrity and authenticity are very evident characteristics of Alasdair's and this runs throughout the members of this fantastic business academy. Whatever you're struggling with, you feel that Alasdair is there to help and guide you. I appreciate and value the truth and the direct nature and opinions of Alasdair and the team as I believe if we are here to provoke changes in ourselves for the better then sometimes we have to confront those things that are holding us back - Reyhan Hakki

Printed in Great Britain
by Amazon